Date Due

APR 2 3 1979	MAR 3 1 1994	
OCT 1 5 1984		
OCT 16 1984	JUL 0 6 2006	
MAR 1 1 1985		
MAR 2 5 1985	JUN 2	
MAR 2 1 1985		
APR 0 4 1985		
MAR 2 9 1985		
APR 2 9 1986		
APR 2 8 1986		
JAN 2 1987		
DEC 1 7 1986		

162

The Assassination
of Pierre Laporte

The Assassination of Pierre Laporte

Behind the October '70 Scenario

Pierre Vallières

Translated by Ralph Wells

James Lorimer & Company, Publishers
Toronto 1977

Published simultaneously in French by Les Editions Québec-Amérique, Montréal

ISBN 0-88862-136-1 paper
ISBN 0-88862-137-X cloth

Cover design: Don Fernley

James Lorimer & Company, Publishers
Egerton Ryerson Memorial Building
35 Britain Street
Toronto

Printed and bound in Canada

Canadian Cataloguing in Publication Data

Vallières, Pierre, 1938-
    The assassination of Pierre Laporte

French ed. published under title: "l'Exécution" de Pierre Laporte.

ISBN 0-88862-137-X bd. ISBN 0-88862-136-1 pa.

1. Laporte, Pierre, 1921-1970. 2. Quebec (Province) - History - October crisis, 1970.* 3. Statesmen - Quebec (Province) - Biography. I. Title

FC2925.1.L35V3513   971.4'04'0924   C77-001202-7
F1053.L35V3513

For Jacques Ferron

CONTENTS

Chronology

1970

October 5 British Trade Commissioner James Cross is kidnapped at his Montreal residence by four gunmen identified later as members of the "Liberation Cell" of the Front de Libération du Québec.

October 10 Pierre Laporte, Quebec's labour minister and deputy premier, is kidnapped in front of his St. Lambert home by four gunmen belonging to the self-styled "Chénier Fund-Raising Cell" of the FLQ.

October 15 Thousands of troops are rushed to Montreal and other centres across Quebec under terms of the National Defence Act.

October 16 The Canadian government proclaims the War Measures Act, suspending civil liberties and banning the FLQ. About 250 Québécois are interned without charges in a single day, another 250 later.

October 17 Laporte's body is found in the trunk of the car used a week earlier to kidnap him, abandoned at the heavily guarded St. Hubert air base.

December 2 The Canadian Parliament passes the Public Order Act, extending most provisions of the War Measures Act for five months.

December 3 Lawyers arrange the release of James Cross in return for a military flight to Cuba for his kidnappers.

December 28 Three suspects in the Laporte assassination are arrested in a farmhouse south of Montreal.

1971

January 4 The armed forces' intervention in Quebec comes to an end.

July 31 Remaining charges against 32 suspects are dropped. Of the 497 persons interned under the emergency laws, fewer than 20 are convicted, most of them pleading guilty to reduced charges in return for light sentences.

It is my hope that some day the full details of the intelligence upon which the government acted can be made public, because until that day comes the people of Canada will not be able fully to appreciate the course of action which has been taken by the government.

John Turner, October 16, 1970

In spite of very strict orders from the authorities . . . the people of Quebec will eventually learn the truth about the worst scandal in their history.

A Montreal city policeman, January 1972

PREFACE

Five years ago, I wrote in *Choose!* that, in spite of the Trudeau government's fierce opposition, the rise to power of the Quebec *indépendantistes* through democratic means seemed absolutely impossible to prevent.* I added, however, that this prospect would not in any way deter federal authorities from seeking new excuses to repeat the excesses of October 1970. In their eyes, the Quebec independence movement, whatever shade of ideology and tactics it might adopt, has represented since 1960, nothing less than "a permanent conspiracy against democracy."†

On the evening of November 15, 1976, like hundreds of thousands of Québécois, I realized with deep emotion the full impact and significance of a collective awakening. The voters had just raised the independence issue to the level of negotiations between two democratically elected governments — one in Quebec that unexpectedly scored a clean sweep at the expense of the submissive and corrupt Liberals, and another in Ottawa that immediately reaffirmed, six years after the War Measures Act of October 1970, that Canada is indivisible.

* Pierre Vallières, *Choose!*, new press, 1972, p. 9 (English translation of *L'urgence de choisir*, Editions Parti Pris, 1971)
† "Le vrai complot" ("The Real Plot"), Louis Martin, *Le Magazine Maclean*, November 1975

This truly historic turning point, when the Québécois people seemingly conquered two centuries of fear and subjection, released high hopes in Quebec. But it should not blind the Québécois to the implacable determination of federal authorities to preserve "Canadian unity" and to uphold by any means the principles proclaimed in the White Paper on Canadian Defence Policy, issued in August 1971;* the same principles that were invoked in 1970, when Quebec was subjected to military occupation and an unprecedented psychological battering.

It is not being alarmist or paranoid to recall the opposition of Western countries to all forms of "secession" within that so-called Free World whose borders are guaranteed by the NATO treaty.

Nor is it being defeatist to acknowledge the declared hostility of the United States to any political proposal that might involve "a risk of balkanization" along its borders.

Pierre Trudeau is not the only one today who believes that this risk is greater than ever and that, one way or another, it must be eliminated. It is not surprising that, soon after the Parti Québécois' election victory, the prime minister of Canada met the American ambassador in Ottawa to discuss the danger of a "Cuba of the north" being created, and the short- and long-term measures needed to counter this threat once and for all.

Immediately after this informal summit meeting, Trudeau prompted his cabinet colleagues to endorse publicly once more the hard line he has always taken toward Quebec. Then, on November 19, he travelled to Montreal to meet selected business executives and Quebec officials of the federal Liberal Party.

Without even waiting for the new government of Quebec to be sworn in, Trudeau was setting out again on the path of confrontation.

While it is impossible at this stage to predict the strategy that

* Queen's Printer, Ottawa, August 24, 1971

the Parti Québécois government will adopt in its dealings with the federal government, it would be an unforgivable mistake to ignore or underrate the fact that Ottawa feels bound to frustrate the triumph of that strategy at all costs. This does not mean, of course, that a federal victory is inevitable. It does mean that the battle won by the Parti Québécois on November 15 compels the central government to launch a counter-offensive. Thus, the "constitutional talks" of the last fifteen years are bound to give way to a full-scale political crisis. If this were not the case, the Québécois would be fooling themselves when they assume these days that they are making a giant political leap forward.

We must not forget that by choosing in an election a government committed to making us "masters in our own house," we have chosen at the same time to break completely with the collusions that accompany the status quo in any subjection, be it constitutional or economic or both.

The struggle for freedom begun in 1960 by a handful of Québécois has now, to the amazement of English Canada and the United States, taken hold of the best political tool of all — a state. It is the same provincial apparatus that federal authorities considered sufficiently threatened by "the separatists" in 1970 to impose the War Measures Act.

And yet, the federalists were in power at all levels of government six years ago. But the twenty-three per cent share of the popular vote garnered by the independence party in the April 29, 1970, election was enough — as I argue in this book — to trigger the mobilization of the armed forces.

Now that the "separatist threat", far from being crushed, has assumed power in Quebec, what can we expect?

Let us not fool ourselves. The constitutional legitimacy of the November 15, 1976 election and Premier René Lévesque's government certainly cannot be challenged. On the other hand, the legitimacy of the Parti Québécois' objectives *is* challenged vigorously by the divine right of the keepers of the Canadian constitution, which the British Parliament bequeathed to us in 1867 without consulting the people.

Less than one week after the Parti Québécois election victory and despite all the moderate statements by the party's leadership, the spectre of "destabilization tactics", reminiscent of those used in Chile, was already looming on the horizon.

In fact, such tactics are not new. To cite only a few instances since Trudeau went to Ottawa, we have had the odious economic blackmail directed at the government of Daniel Johnson (which led to the notorious and humiliating statement extracted from the vacationing premier in Hawaii in October 1967);* the forced resignation of the autonomist Jean Lesage as Quebec Liberal leader in August 1969; the spectacular use of Brink's armored trucks by the Royal Trust Co. on the eve of the 1970 election to transfer "securities" to Toronto; the creation in Ottawa of the May 7 Committee soon after that election (see Chapter I and Appendix I); and the events of October 1970. All these attacks on Quebec improved the political fortunes of the Trudeau government.

After the War Measures onslaught, most people in English Canada assumed that the issue of "Quebec separatism" had been settled for good. The 1973 Quebec election seemed to confirm the total victory of Canadian centralism, and many English-speaking Canadians felt that the time had come to dispense with even the temporary drawbacks of window-dressing bilingualism. They were getting ready to let Trudeau know clearly that his role as the "saviour" of Canadian unity had come to an end and that he could go home.

* This statement, which indicated that Johnson favoured a new Canadian constitution rather than Quebec independence, was published by *La Presse* on October 4, 1967, after Paul Desmarais (chairman of the Power Corporation conglomerate and owner of the Montreal daily *La Presse)* flew to Hawaii to urge the premier to reject separatism.

Then the Parti Québécois won the 1976 election with a comfortable majority. Shocked, certain English-speaking Canadians accused Trudeau of having misled them and having failed miserably to achieve his mission. But at the same time, they remained convinced that, with or without Trudeau, Ottawa must take a firm position, now more than ever.

Will this situation provide the leader of "French Power" with the challenge he needs to proclaim himself once more as the right man for the job? I could not help asking myself that question — and many others — while completing this book on the October Crisis and the assassination of Pierre Laporte.

I remembered this statement, among others, made by Trudeau: "To all Canadians who believe in democracy, Pierre Laporte is a martyr. His death must not be a pointless tragedy. We must see to it that it becomes a landmark in the crusade for Canadian unity." And this statement by Robert Bourassa: "He gave his life for the defence of fundamental rights." They spoke on October 18, 1970.

At the same time, I recalled Trudeau's comments on November 15, 1976: "The Parti Québécois has no mandate to separate Quebec from Canada nor to change the constitution."

Are the events of 1970 bad memories that would best be forgotten? I do not believe so. On the contrary, it is high time to shed light on "the facts about the October Crisis and its causes," as the Parti Québécois put it in a motion calling for a public inquiry.*

As the playwright Jean-Claude Germain would say, if Quebec wants to make history instead of submitting to it, it must never again be "the country whose motto is 'I Forget'."

This essay deals with one of the darkest periods of Quebec-

---

* Debates of the Quebec National Assembly, October 30, 1970. This request was repeated many times, notably in 1975.

Ottawa confrontation, yet also one of the most significant and least understood.

* * * * *

I have divided this analysis of the causes, deeds and consequences of October 1970 into four chapters.

Chapter I deals with the preparation of the crisis inside the armed forces, the police and the federal political structures. It describes how and why the October 1970 kidnappings were foreseen and welcomed by the authorities, which controlled their timing and unfolding with almost "mathematical" precision.*

Chapter II describes how Operation Essay, the code name chosen by the Canadian Armed Forces for the 1970 "manoeuvres", unfolded from October 5, 1970, to January 5, 1971. These military "manoeuvres" were aimed at testing the army's role and effectiveness in a direct intervention in "civil disturbances", while at the same time serving the political purpose of deterring the Québécois once and for all from aspiring (even unconsciously) to independence.

Chapter III, the longest, deals more specifically with the assassination of Pierre Laporte, which came soon after the proclamation of the War Measures Act and served to legitimize it. Many facts relating to the minister's death are disclosed here for the first time, while several others were revealed in 1973 and 1975. Even though many of the circumstances surrounding Laporte's kidnapping, sequestration and death have been covered up and even though many important witnesses have been sworn to secrecy, an examination of the facts now on record leads to conclusions that are quite different from the "official version" fabricated to suit the needs of the federal war on separatism. This examination of the facts raises serious questions

---

* Gérard Pelletier, *The October Crisis,* McClelland & Stewart, 1971, p. 127
(English translation of *La crise d'octobre,* Editions du Jour, 1971)

about the truth of government statements that have been made until now about the Laporte case. These facts warrant a new coroner's inquest or public inquiry.

A group of the late minister's friends made no mistake when they wrote, in a letter to *Le Devoir* published October 30, 1970, that history ultimately would judge, not the FLQ, but "our governments, certain ministers and Liberal politicians." For, whatever roles third parties (self-styled FLQ members or others) may have played in Laporte's sequestration and death, the decisive role in the case was played by the then-authorities.

The people of Quebec have never been manipulated and hoodwinked as odiously as they were in October 1970. This manipulation affected and continues to affect the political reflexes of the Québécois. The fourth and last chapter is intended to assess precisely this impact and to raise the following question — if new federal aggression occurs, will the Québécois be better able to face up to it than they were in 1970? Do we run the risk of again witnessing, powerless and frustrated, the negation of "all our chances for a future," as René Lévesque put it on October 16, 1970?

Certainly, we have been cautioned since 1970 that an "implacable logic" guides the policies and actions of the central government,* especially when it is convinced that a crisis is "inevitable in the relatively near future."† We are forewarned that if there is again a federal response to Quebec's designs for independence, it will not for very long be confined to words.

On November 15, 1976, we finally regained our sense of solidarity and pride. The events of 1970 did not cripple us. The future of Quebec remains worthy of the efforts that have been exerted ever since 1960 on the road to independence. But the final victory remains a long way off.

Ibid., p. 131
†*Ibid.*, p. 133

Federal authorities will do everything they can to set a trap for Quebec. In this connection, the lessons than can be drawn from the events of October 1970 are more timely than ever.

When it comes to the future of Quebec, the central government has a rather peculiar notion of the democratic process. For instance, after the Liberal victory in the April 1970 Quebec election, when the federal politicians were proclaiming that ''separatism'' was dead and buried, Ottawa was secretly preparing for the proclamation of the War Measures Act. Today, secrecy prevails again as the federal government prepares its counter-offensives in the name of the indivisibility of Canada.

Pierre Vallières,
Saint-Mathias-de-Bonneterre,
November 26, 1976,
The day when the first Quebec government dedicated to independence took office.

Author's Note

I wish to thank all those who assisted me in the preparation of this book — journalists, persons active in politics, public officials and others — by granting me lengthy interviews or giving me access to their files. I have also drawn from unpublished official documents I have obtained from various sources since 1975 and from hundreds of pages of research notes compiled by the CBC television network for its documentary *The October Crisis* broadcast in October 1975. In addition, I consulted the stenographic records of the 1970 coroner's inquest into the slaying of Pierre Laporte and of the subsequent murder trials. I reread practically everything about the events of 1970 that was published in Quebec's leading French- and English-language newspapers.

Of course, many facts about October 1970 and the Laporte assassination remain secret. But the information collected and published here for the first time raises disturbing questions and amply demonstrates the need for a thorough public inquiry to establish at last the true circumstances surrounding the imposition of the War Measures Act, the vast military and police operations aimed at crippling the Quebec independence movement, and the week-long ordeal of Pierre Laporte.

Pierre Valliéres

1

PREPARING THE OCTOBER CRISIS

As Professor Maxwell Cohen stated on October 16, 1970, Quebec had been "a vast laboratory of social change" for a decade. Like many people in the midst of the October Crisis he believed that the overthrow of the established order was an imminent possibility. On that day, he went so far as to describe the chain of events that followed the kidnapping of British diplomat James Cross on October 5, as a real and deliberate attempt by the FLQ to effect "a revolutionary transformation of society."*

Unknown to Professor Cohen, the "crisis" that had just culminated in the proclamation of the War Measures Act by the Trudeau government had been staged-managed meticulously by a "Strategic Operations Centre" in Ottawa.

This chapter describes the political background and strategies that gave rise to the October Crisis. First we set out the strategy of the federal government, planned by a secret group of mandarins in Ottawa. We then deal with the preparations for the crisis by the armed forces, the police, and Liberal politicians in Quebec and Ottawa. After considering the role in the crisis of American authorities, acting through the CIA and other agencies, and the interest of the British, the chapter concludes with a description of

*La Presse, Montreal, October 17, 1970

the media's activities, from the initial total concentration of public attention on the kidnappings to the much more "disciplined" approach following the discovery of Pierre Laporte's body.

The Electric Shock Strategy

The political strategy behind Ottawa's role in the October Crisis was quite simple. Federal authorities were resolved in 1970 to teach the Quebec *indépendantistes* a real lesson, to belt them hard. At the same time, by administering a kind of political shock treatment to the population, they wanted to force the hand of all segments of Quebec society, and extract from them immediately and unequivocally a full disclosure of their long-term political objectives.

Ever since the formation of the Jean Lesage government in 1960, a hesitation waltz between "semi-federalists" and "semi-separatists" had produced endless ideological waffling in Quebec. The federal mandarins considered this absence of a clear-cut polarization between federalism and separatism as a grave threat to the future stability of the federal system. Due to constant shifts among autonomist, separatist and "renewed" federalist positions, English Canadians were left with no definite answer to their standard question: What does Quebec really want?

But the precision and definitiveness you can expect in a collective reply to a major political question depends on the *intensity* with which the public expresses itself. In other words, to obtain a precise answer to this question would require an *intense* collective shock to the political psyche of Quebec. This shock, whatever its nature, would have to be severe enough to provoke an immediate mass response in the shortest possible period of time, so that people's responses would display their true feelings and emotions, and would not be the products of reason or rationalization. And the more intense — and precise — the response, the less likelihood there would be of a misunderstanding between the people of Quebec and English Canadians. This view of political life, and the desire to smear the "separatist" leadership lay at the root of the October Crisis in 1970.

The imposition of the War Measures Act during the October Crisis was the big shock devised by the federal strategists, who were concerned not just with their immediate problems but were also looking well into the future.

In 1964, well before the founding of the Parti Québécois, Pierre Trudeau was already equating the Quebec independence movement with a dangerous conspiracy whose single purpose was to undermine democracy and freedom, both inseparable from "Canadian unity" in his mind. Trudeau was also deeply worried about the autonomist leanings of the Lesage government which, in his view, stimulated separatist subversion. Once in Ottawa, he quickly showed his preference for confrontation and provocation (by attending the St. Jean Baptiste Day parade in 1968, for instance) to clarify a political situation. But, until Robert Bourassa became leader of the Quebec Liberal Party, no one in Quebec seemed willing to play along with this as an overall strategy for dealing with the Quebec question.

In the April 1970 election, the independence party Trudeau had dismissed as "a particle" made an unexpected breakthrough in its first election campaign, by capturing one-quarter of the popular vote. In Ottawa, the brain trust immediately swung into action. The government was anxious to find out quickly and surely whether the pre-independence upsurge amounted simply to a political accident, or whether it reflected an irreversible trend. The United States and NATO were just as anxious as Ottawa to know the answer.

Putting the question to the Québécois through traditional means (such as opinion polls) would have been a waste of time. Many "federalists" were expressing interest in separatist arguments following the emergence of the independence option in Quebec. Nationalism was infecting everyone, generating all sorts of demands for change. These ranged from a new division of constitutional powers and the associate states concept, to the Parti Québécois program (a sovereign Quebec state linked with Canada in an economic association) and calls from other groups for a socialist revolution. In the eyes of the horrified Trudeau government, all Québécois appeared more-or-less as accomplices of subversion, possessed by a diabolical determination to stop submitting or adapting to the rigid and centralizing framework of "Canadian unity". The collective erosion of a sense of belonging to an "indivisible" Canada was, in their view, not only pulling Quebec away from the constitutional framework, but away from democracy as well.

On May 7, 1970, one week after the Quebec election, the federal cabinet set up a special committee, one of whose functions was to determine the circumstances in which the Québécois could be jolted by a political bombshell (See Appendix I.)* The FLQ, which was being watched very closely by the RCMP, would serve as the detonator. This time, the "bomb" would be the proclamation of the War Measures Act in the middle of the

---

* "Ottawa began to look at War Measures well before crisis", *The Globe and Mail,* Toronto, copyright, December 23, 1971. The article disclosed that the federal cabinet decided on May 7, 1970 to create an interdepartmental committee to consider "steps to be taken in the event the War Measures Act comes into force by reason of insurrection." Questioned in the House of Commons, Prime Minister Trudeau acknowledged that the *Globe and Mail* article was based on secret cabinet documents leaked to the newspaper's Ottawa bureau in violation of official secrecy regulations. The May 7 committee was formed a few days after the Quebec election in which the Parti Québécois made its first breakthrough and after the Kent State University tragedy in which the Ohio National Guard killed four demonstrating students.

night. This would really show whether, in a state of shock, the Québécois were ready to "fight" if need be to win their independence, or whether they would rather denounce separatism.

As for the media, they would serve to "plug in" the whole population to these events and, when the time was ripe, provide instant transmission of the shock. In this way, under the guise of a do-or-die struggle between the FLQ and the authorities, the October Crisis would enable Ottawa to carry out a massive electronic referendum and gauge the true strength of public sympathy for independence.

The May 7 committee set up by the cabinet obviously knew that the media would report and dramatize the crisis developments. It also knew that this instant transmission of news and rumours would quickly create the climate of anxiety needed to proceed as far as possible with the "organized escalation" of tension in the collective consciousness. Of course, there would be various distortions, since any society is highly complex, and people are vulnerable to this kind of manipulation. But, for the Trudeau government, the exercise was worth the trouble. Besides, the total surprise provoked by this electric shock would give the government the advantage and prevent its opponents from reacting effectively. And the government could amplify or reduce the cumulative impact of the crisis in line with its designs.

The implementation of this manipulative operation was assigned to a group of politicians, police and military officials who made up the Strategic Operations Centre (SOC), which set up headquarters at 67 Sparks Street in Ottawa. SOC comprised officials from the Prime Minister's Office, including Jim Davey, Robin Bourne, Fernand Cadieux and Jean-Pierre Mongeau, Jean-Pierre Goyer (named Solicitor-General, and thus responsible for the RCMP, a few weeks later), Arnold Masters (a Montreal shipping executive and former aide to Bryce Mackasey), representatives of the armed forces and RCMP, and a few others. The existence of SOC (which apparently grew out of the May 7 Committee) was not disclosed until October 1975, when the CBC network aired a television documentary on the 1970 crisis. SOC reported directly to Pierre Trudeau and Marc Lalonde, then his Principal Secretary.

In brief, what happened was this. For months, members of the May 7 Committee collected detailed files on the FLQ activists' plans. They let them get organized. During the summer of 1970, the National Defence College in Kingston, Ontario, conducted "war games" to teach high-ranking officers how to respond to political kidnappings, as the CBC documentary revealed. When the time was ripe, all that remained to be done was to mobilize the public's attention solidly around the "FLQ exploits" and then to transform this prolonged attention into ever-increasing tension. From the kidnapping of an "anglais" to the assassination of a "French Canadian", from verbal demagoguery to military occupation, this rising tension would force each Québécois to take a stand *for* or *against* this "subversive conspiracy that constitutes separatism, from the PQ to the FLQ," as Jean Marchand put it on October 16, 1970, and for or against the mortal danger of nationalism, which threatened the very existence of the government of Quebec.

The Candid Confessions of Gérard Pelletier

The account by former cabinet minister Gérard Pelletier in his book on the October Crisis offers indirect confirmation of this view of how the October Crisis came about. Says Pelletier: "The role of a government is doubtless to administer the interests and promote the values of the community. And it is very much more. Every government has a mission to help bring about the society of the future; to foresee and bring about necessary change. . . ."*

Further on, Pelletier adds: "There is something mathematical in the unfolding of a crisis of this nature."** Then, referring to the repression of 1970, carried out in the name of an established order that was not really threatened at all, the ex-journalist and Trudeau crony writes in his learned style: "The real challenge lies in refusing to deviate from the *initial trajectory,* in not using repression for ends other than those *precise and circums-tantial* purposes for which it was invoked." † "The authorities have the choice of drawing *more or less* from this arsenal and of using *for a longer or shorter time* the instruments at hand." ††
The techniques "vary chiefly in their *intensity* and in their *duration,*" but they must *always* "move tangentially to the [predetermined] vicious circle of repression." ★ (Italics added.)

In short, as long as one does not lose control over the machine, "a crisis of this nature" can be programmed mathematically to "bring about the society of the future." That is the future selected by those in power, of course.

In the same book, Pelletier describes the performance of the Trudeau government in 1970 as having an "implacable logic" ★★ within which "the parts [were] allocated *in advance.*" ⁂ Such "political determinism," of course, "inevitably engenders a certain number of injustices" and "it can even be added that . . . the first victims of [these] injustices will come principally from opposition circles." ✩✩

It now seems clear that Pelletier's attempt to justify the

---

* Gérard Pelletier, *The October Crisis,* p. 29
** *Ibid.,* p. 127
† *Ibid.,* p. 129
†† *Ibid.,* p. 129
★ *Ibid.,* p. 129
★★ *Ibid.,* p. 131
⁂ *Ibid.,* p. 131
✩✩ *Ibid.,* pp. 141 and 143

government's role in the October Crisis was directly inspired by the mandarins at the Strategic Operations Centre.

With cool audacity, both during and after the events of 1970, Trudeau and his team blamed the kidnappers (that is, a total of ten persons) for the trap they had themselves set for the Québécois. They blamed the "extremists" for what the government itself had decided to do.

The shock treatment used was not just developed over a few months in Ottawa but had in fact been worked out over many years, not just by the political authorities, but also by the armed forces and the police.

The Armed Forces' Preparations

As one might expect, the basic ideas behind the 1970 military strike came from American military and intelligence planners and strategists. For the past thirty years, the U.S. has exercised through the NATO and NORAD treaties a virtual trusteeship over the Canadian Armed Forces and their capability to intervene at home and abroad.

In order to achieve their main objective regarding Canada — the "continental rationalization" of economic, political and military activities — and their other major foreign and domestic policy objectives, the Americans have long seized on the enormous advantages they could derive from the use of sophisticated electronic hardware, computers, and models of how societies operate.

In the late 1940s, American universities developed data processing technology and began popularizing the multiple uses of computers. The experts in this field realized that the new technology would have a major impact on society. They showed government agencies and multinational corporations that computers could tie in with telecommunications systems and mass media, giving a few officials a virtual monopoly over detailed information about a given problem. They argued that this gave government bureaucrats and corporate executives the power to make "functional" decisions and long-range forecasts through the use of scenarios.

Pierre Trudeau, who attended Harvard University about this time, became an enthusiastic convert to this "functional approach". He referred to it repeatedly in *Cité Libre* and in the "Manifesto for a Functional Public Policy" that he, Marc Lalonde and several other Montreal intellectuals published in 1964. In recent years, computer experts have developed highly sophisticated "crisis management" techniques that bypass the normal democratic decision-making process and concentrate power in the hands of a handful of people at the top. These key officials wield enormous influence because they receive a massive flow of facts that usually are not available to legislators, civil servants and the public.

Thus, during the kidnap crisis in 1970, Jim Davey and other computer enthusiasts in the Prime Minister's Office set up SOC and the so-called East Block War Room on Parliament Hill. These nerve centers, which operated under tight security and to which the Quebec government and police forces were denied access, were plugged into special telephone circuits, telecommunications, news agency wires, military communications and government data banks. The "war rooms" even received tapes of Quebec radio and television programming from the Canadian Radio-Television Commission in an apparent violation of CRTC rules. This sort of concentration of information and power in the hands of a few non-elected officials saps the rights of the individual and leads toward the creation of a completely controlled social system.

Particularly important has been the modernization of the social apparatus of control and repression by means of data-processing systems and the centralization of all "law enforcement" agencies through a single co-ordinating body. In Canada, this co-ordinating body is called the National Emergency Planning Establishment. This group serves to "reduce to a minimum the number of unforeseen crises" by means of "creative planning" based on computer systems.* Such a centre could, at least in theory, completely fabricate a state of crisis designed to justify for public opinion the testing of the entire machinery for intervention (that is, repression) in peacetime.

For the armed forces, the October Crisis was a military exercise code-named Operation Essay, as we shall see further on. † For political purposes, this operation was an attempt to reduce the elements of uncertainty and risk that the Quebec independence movement represented, as it still does, for the future of an "indivisible Canada". At the same time, the Trudeau team intended to "give birth" to the "Canadian future" of Quebec society, as Gérard Pelletier later put it; a future in which the parts were cast in advance by the constitution and in which social and political behaviour had to remain functional, that is, controlled in a "mathematical" way.

Without the logistic support of the armed forces, this brand of social functionalism would have been nothing more than a kind of fascist utopianism. But the armed forces are only too happy to co-operate with a policy aimed at making human choices functional and abolishing a challenge to the very system that they are assigned to maintain unchanged. For, in North America, the armed forces have been given the mission of opposing enemies within as effectively as they would foreign enemies.

---

* Report of the Study Group on the Strengthening of Crisis Intervention Machinery in the Federal Administration, October 15, 1974.

† This exercise was called Opération Essai in French, the name implying that it was a trial run or a dress rehearsal.

In the sixties, military planners in the U.S. and Canada began drafting fictitious scenarios for insurrections, civil disturbances, and so on. These scenarios had to be tested sometime, as apparently happened at Kent State University, to correct, if necessary, any weaknesses in this "home defence". In the U.S., all these experimental operations were code-named Garden Plot.*

In 1970, the Canadian forces came up with Operation Essay. Details of this operation remained secret until 1975, when researchers for the CBC TV program about the October Crisis obtained a full account from military sources. Through a planned provocation, it was designed to meet three objectives. † These were: perfecting the repressive machinery across the country; centralizing all available data on subversion (and more particularly, information on "separatist subversion"); and bolstering Canadian unity by disorganizing and dislocating as much as possible the groups promoting Quebec nationalism. The third objective was only partially achieved because of resistance to the mass raids that began spreading among French-speaking officers and men. This resulted in a purge in 1971, when many "separatists" were discharged from the Canadian forces on various pretexts, such as health reasons.

The original plan for Operation Essay called for an all-out sweep, which would have resulted in the internment of the leading figures in the Parti Québécois, the labour federations and all social groups deemed "irresponsible". In short, all those who, in the words of Gérard Pelletier in *The October Crisis*, showed through their opposition to the federal government's actions, an "indulgence," an "unacknowledged sympathy for the values and methods" of FLQ subversion.††

* "Bringing the War Home", *New Times*, New York, November 28, 1975, pp. 18-24

† Details of this operation remained secret until 1975, when CBC researchers obtained the information from high-ranking military sources.

†† Gérard Pelletier, *op. cit.*, p. 159

The origins of Operation Essay go back to 1960. That year, the army prepared its first contingency plans for the suppression of potential "insurrections" in Quebec. This task was carried out by the Planning and Operations Section of the Quebec Command. Shortly before, the election of the reformist team led by Jean Lesage had put an end to more than twenty years of political and social stability in the province.

This turning point, known as the Quiet Revolution, created the risk of civil disturbances in the army's view. Of course, there was no quesion then of subjecting the people of Quebec to the kind of mass media shock treatment that we witnessed in 1970. But the army planned to be ready to face any eventuality.

To test its plan, the army sent a battalion of 1,000 troops to St. Vincent de Paul Penitentiary during a riot in 1961. Then, beginning in 1963, when the Front de Libération du Québec manifested itself, the army set up liaison with the Quebec police forces and their anti-subversive squads. Operation Revolt, launched by the Pentagon in 1962 to study the social changes under way in Quebec, called for such liaison.* For a long time their military intelligence services had been co-operating closely with those of the RCMP. After 1963, especially during the 1964-65 period, this co-operation spread to the Quebec Police Force (commanded by former RCMP officers) and to the Montreal police anti-terrorist squad. The links between the military and the police rapidly became institutional and operational, following the model established in the U.S. in preparation for the quelling of urban race riots.

As early as 1965, the Canadian army not only had detailed information about how the FLQ operated but also about who belonged to it.†

* The existence of the U.S. Army operation code-named Project Revolt did not become known until late February 1966 when disclosures by Toronto newspapers sparked a series of questions in the House of Commons.

In 1966, a major change took place in the armed forces — the three services were integrated and a Mobile Command was established. This new command was given responsibility for all future operations on Canadian soil and more specifically, for operations aimed at putting down potential insurrections in Quebec. The Mobile Command headquarters was therefore set up in Quebec, on federal territory at the St. Hubert air base.

The same year that the Mobile Command was created, Quebec *indépendantistes* entered candidates in a provincial election for the first time. The Liberal government was defeated and the new premier of Quebec, Daniel Johnson, adopted a policy of "equality or independence" toward Ottawa. Lester B. Pearson placed Pierre Trudeau in charge of constitutional talks. Two years later, several pro-independence groups joined forces in the Parti Québécois.

Beginning in 1966, all the military operational plans were revised and reshaped in line with the changed political situation and the armed forces reorganization. The plans were divided into two general categories. "A" Category deals with operations carried out as part of regular NATO manoeuvres and these operations are code numbered from 600 to 699. "B" Category, carrying code numbers from 200 to 299, deals with the prevention and repression of civil unrest, and aid to the civil power during natural disasters and oil spills.

One of the "B" Category plans drawn up in 1966 to protect the internal security of Canada was given the code number 210 (it was part of a set of twenty-three such plans for intervention). The objective of Plan 210 was to control agitation and agitators everywhere in Canada, but more particularly in Quebec. In 1966, all "anti-terrorist" operations were already being handled

† *Background on Military Role in October Crisis,* an unpublished study prepared for the 1975 CBC documentary *The October Crisis,* p. 4. This study is hereinafter referred to as CBC, *Background on Military Role.*

by the Mobile Command headquarters, which could rely hence-
forth on 25,000 troops and on the various police forces, which
had been completely reorganized in line with the military plans.

Within the ambit of Plan 210, directly or through the use of
specialized police units, military intelligence proceeded systematically to infiltrate the *indépendantiste* circles, the labour
movement, the universities, and so on. They also infiltrated the
political parties and even the executive council of Quebec. One is
reminded of a 1968 press conference at which Premier Daniel
Johnson charged angrily that an electronic eavesdropping device
had been planted in his own office.*

The army not only monitored agitation, it provoked it. Some
of its agents were involved in demonstrations and labour dis-
putes. Monitoring all levels of Quebec's institutions, the Mobile
Command officers were scrutinizing, analyzing, making projec-
tions, building scenarios, provoking "significant" incidents and
preparing the counter-offensive against separatism.

One of the tactics they used was to identify separatism with the
FLQ and, through it, with a vast international conspiracy to
establish communism in North America through revolutionary
means. In this plot, Quebec was supposed to become "a Cuba of
the north."

In 1964 and 1965, an FBI sergeant named Roy Wood implicated several Québécois in a conspiracy he devised to blow up
"freedom monuments" such as the Statue of Liberty and the
Washington Monument. The undercover sergeant had posed as a
member of the Black Nationalist Front.†

From 1966 to 1970, military and police agents of the anti-

---

* Charles Drury, then a federal cabinet minister, admitted on September 18,
1972 that the military intelligence service had gathered data on labour and
political groups after René Lévesque issued copies of an army intelligence
report on officials of the Confederation of National Trade Unions.

† Gustave Morf, *Terror in Québec,* Clarke Irwin & Co., Toronto, 1970, pp.
77-79

subversive campaign played an important role as provocateurs on many occasions. They were involved in particular in the St. Jean Baptiste parade in Montreal on June 24, 1968; the sacking of the Sir George Williams University computer centre; the "McGill français" operation; the Montreal police strike on October 7, 1969, and the fire at the Murray Hill bus garage that same night. Through agents who infiltrated the Company of Young Canadians, the most active demonstrators were identified and placed under surveillance.* These included most of those who formed the 1970 FLQ cells.

The proliferation of demonstrations in Montreal, especially between 1968 and 1970, created the appearance of a basis for a "revolutionary threat", which was compared during the October Crisis to a deliberate attempt to bring about a coup d'état. Unknown to the demonstrators, however, the development of "revolutionary" consciousness and action among the Québécois was manipulated by the armed forces and the various police forces active in Quebec who were in touch with the groups in question and who knew the activists involved.

Despite this "revolutionary threat", about which the politicians in power were warned gravely by the armed forces, the military were not able to intervene as they wished until October 1970.

During the Montreal police strike and the rioting that ensued on October 7, 1969, Premier Jean-Jacques Bertrand (an autonomist, after all) hesitated too long before acceding to the Mobile Command's exhortations. When he finally called in the

---

* Lucien Saulnier, former chairman of the City of Montreal executive committee, confirmed this in an interview with *Le Jour* in November 1975. He said that when he demanded a public inquiry into the activities of "professional agitators" in the Company of Young Canadians in 1969, he was told by the federal cabinet that such an inquiry would be against national security requirements because many of the "extremists" in the youth corps were in fact undercover agents.

troops, the disturbances were dying down. General Roland Reid, who had been pressuring Bertrand in vain for several hours, went home fuming that night. (The same general, incidentally, was in charge of the $100-million display of military might during the 1976 Olympics at Montreal.)

Mobile Command, incensed over the "politicians' stupidity", set up a new section to deal with "civil emergency situations." Called the Civil Emergencies Section, this unit was to move into the third floor of the Quebec Police Force headquarters on Parthenais Street in Montreal in the early stages of the October Crisis. From there, the authorities were informed and guided before making political decisions during the crisis.

The political functions of the Civil Emergencies Section were considerable. Among other things, it had to seal off from the decision-making process those politicians deemed too indulgent or too soft. To achieve this, the power to make political decisions had to be concentrated in very few hands. In Ottawa, Trudeau's rise to power had given the armed forces full satisfaction in this regard. In Montreal, Mayor Jean Drapeau was watched closely by the city legal director, Michel Côté, who was to assume control over the Combined Anti-Terrorist (CAT) squad on June 7, 1970. In Quebec, persons loyal to federal functionalism had to assume power. This was achieved on April 29, 1970.

Before the election on that date, the armed forces feared that in spite of everything, the rise of the *indépendantistes* might jeopardize the election outcome they had foreseen. By "coincidence", a feeling suddenly spread that "something was in the wind."* The Civil Emergencies Section circulated reports that there was "a strong likelihood of serious trouble in Quebec" because of the election. One report warned in particular that violent incidents might erupt in polling stations on election day. The armed forces even considered intervening in Quebec on

* CBC, *op. cit.*, pp. 6-9

April 29 to "protect" democratic voting. But the Brink's gambit made the intervention unnecessary.

The federalists were nevertheless elected with a clear majority in Quebec. All that remained was to make the new justice minister, Jérôme Choquette, completely receptive to the military views. Of course, this "emotional and naive" new minister was not expected to know and understand everything, but simply to be good enough, when the time came, to legalize Operation Essay, designed to thwart the "revolutionary plot".

Choquette graciously agreed to meet armed forces representatives to establish the "facilities and arrangements" required for the intervention of troops in case of an emergency.* By the late summer of 1970, everything was ready, and meetings between the armed forces and the police forces involved were taking place on a weekly, and sometimes daily, basis.

In February and June, 1970, Montreal police broke up two attempted kidnappings. The plans and even the manifesto of the 1970 FLQ wave were made public. Politicians received reports mentioning the "probability" of kidnappings in the fall and the possibility of "political assassinations".† In Ottawa, the May 7 Committee had given the green light to the "October Crisis" operation. Mobile Command therefore put its forces in a state of preparedness. The RCMP and the CAT squad did likewise.

By late August 1970, the launching of Operation Essay was imminent. All that remained was for the FLQ to go into action.

When the first kidnapping (that of the diplomat James Cross) took place on October 5, there was no surprise among the military and the police, which had expected that kidnapping on September 28! A "red alert" had been flashed on the 28th, putting everyone on a war footing. (Many *indépendantistes*

Ibid., p. 10
†*Ibid.*, p. 11

had also been informed in advance that "a major offensive" was being prepared.)

In October 1970 the impression was fostered that law enforcement agencies were completely unprepared to deal with "this unprecented type of situation." In fact, they were dangerously well prepared.

The Police Preparations

The policemen in the Combined Anti-Terrorist squad had long been waiting for the chance to swing into action. Created in 1964, this squad had been reorganized and reinforced many times since then. The army had played a big role in these reorganizations by providing, among other things, specialized training for policemen in the control of civil disturbances, intelligence techniques and undercover infiltration.

Michel Côté, a loyal ally of the armed forces, the RCMP and director of the legal department of the City of Montreal, was secretly appointed as the effective chief of CAT in June 1970. The squad's headquarters were located on the third floor of an old building on St. Dominique Street, near the Jean Talon produce market in Montreal.

As mentioned previously, Montreal city policemen had uncovered two kidnapping plots, the first in February 1970 and the second in June. During the October Crisis, most of the policemen in the Montreal and suburban forces except the city detectives belonging to CAT (along with men from the RCMP and the Quebec Police Force) were to be diverted away from significant investigations and relegated to diversionary tasks.

The success of Operation Essay required that, as was the case within Mobile Command, only a limited number of policemen be informed about the "manoeuvres" being planned. This situation was the source of the deep discontent that Montreal and Quebec policemen have since voiced over the police handling of the events of 1970.

From 1963 to 1970, the anti-subversive squad had compiled an ever-increasing number of detailed files on activists, most of whom lived in Montreal. Beginning in 1968, it prepared at the request of federal authorities, precise profiles of all known FLQ members and of persons likely to become members. During the summer of 1970, it was able to supply the federal cabinet and the May 7 Committee with the names and records of the FLQ members who were preparing the October kidnappings (except, it seems, for Jacques Cossette-Trudel; by a strange coincidence, his father was named to the National Energy Board by the Trudeau cabinet five days before the Cross kidnapping).*

A political, social and psychological study of the 1970 version of the FLQ concluded that a majority of its members were determined to begin their activities as soon as possible; that there was very little risk that they would endanger the lives of their eventual hostages; that their actions up to that point were disting-uished by a high degree of amateurism; finally, that in any event, their activities could be monitored and manipulated through the help of informers who had been planted in the right places, including some with access to the leaders.†

While the evolution of the crisis might not be entirely predict-able, federal authorities, the armed forces, the RCMP, the QPF and the CAT squad could at least monitor the comings and goings of the kidnappers without too much trouble in the early stages.

In June, the contents of the October FLQ manifesto had already been published by some newspapers, following the col-

---

* Unpublished research material for the 1975 CBC documentary *The October Crisis*. René Matte, Social Credit House leader in Ottawa, suggested in a Commons question on April 2, 1976 that RCMP undercover agents infiltrated the FLQ cells in the 1963-70 period.

† Research material for the 1975 CBC documentary *The October Crisis*, unpublished.

lapse of the ''Lanctôt-Marcil operation'' aimed at kidnapping the U.S. consul in Montreal; the FLQ demands were known; and the FLQ's centres of operations had either been dismantled or located by the police, except for the apartment in Montreal North that Cossette-Trudel was to rent in September.

So the FLQ-1970 was under control in October and any element of surprise was entirely lacking.

On October 5, even the journalists knew immediately what was up. Thus, barely one hour after the kidnapping of James Cross, reporter Jean de Guise wrote in *La Presse* that Jacques Lanctôt was probably involved in the case. De Guise made a direct connection between the kidnapping and the foiled attempts of the previous February and June. For the police, of course, not only was this connection a certainty, but the kidnapping had been expected for many months. They had been awaiting this development to take action.

As soon as the expected kidnapping of Cross was reported, Montreal Police Chief Marcel St. Aubin called Michel Côté at 9:10 a.m. that Monday and told him simply, *''C'est arrivé''* (It just happened). Immediately, CAT launched its crisis operation and the armed forces placed their troops on a standby alert.

The first thing police did that morning was to get confused about the address of the Cross residence and rush to the residence of the Greek consul! They lost track of the kidnappers and the ''revolutionary threat'' became a reality.

One of Cross's neighbours, film director Paul Almond, was astonished. How could a kidnapping be pulled off on a street that had been under very tight police surveillance the previous few days? He told reporters about this the same day, but this detail was quickly forgotten.

The Legislative Preparations

At 11:15 a.m. on October 5, police rushed to the Lafontaine Park campus of the University of Quebec in Montreal and picked up four envelopes that had just been dropped off there by the FLQ Liberation Cell for the news media. (Reporters from CKAC arrived too late, even though the FLQ had called the radio station and not the police.)

At the same time, a man who had learned by accident of the plot to kidnap the British diplomat informed a radio station that Jacques Lanctôt was involved. This witness, who was as hostile to separatism as Trudeau can be, had notified police beforehand about the kidnappers' plans. He had no idea that the police and the authorities had known what was afoot well before him, and that these events had been expected for a long time.

In Ottawa, people pretended to be "absolutely surprised." In Montreal, Justice Minister Choquette hastened to convene his first crisis press conference. Detectives from the Combined Anti-Terrorist squad were interviewing known activists with mysterious smiles on their faces. News media mobilized their personnel with surprising feverishness.

At his press conference Choquette revealed that he had just been in touch with the RCMP, the QPF and the CAT squad. His predecessor, Rémi Paul, told reporters that the kidnapping that occurred that morning had been planned since 1969.

Paul, who had projected a forbidding image as justice minister in the previous Union Nationale government, had announced a ten point program to combat Quebec terrorism on August 22, 1969. This program particularly stressed increased surveillance of known and suspected "terrorists".* A short time before, the same Rémi Paul had caught everyone by surprise when he had spoken out in support of the people hanging out at La Maison du

*La Presse, final edition, October 1, 1970

Pêcheur in Perçé (including Paul and Jacques Rose, Francis Simard, Bernard Lortie, Jacques Lanctôt, and others) who were accused of being revolutionaries by the town's prominent citizens. It so happens, as Jacques Ferron pointed out some time later in his newspaper column *(Le Canada francais,* October 24, 1972), that La Maison du Pêcheur was then an excellent observation post for policemen and their informers. And the mayor of Perçé admitted as much in November 1970.

By the time of Paul's 1969 announcement, co-ordination between the military and police intelligence services had become so close that information was being exchanged regularly. The program announced by Paul was aimed primarily at linking the legislators with the military and police intelligence operations. After all, in our system of government, the armed forces and the police are legally subject to political supervision. Appearances thus had to be preserved before anyone had the chance to sound an early warning against the emergence of a state within the state.

Quebec legislators were at that time going through a period of serious instability. Bill 63, which granted parents the right to choose between French and English schools, created divisions within the traditional parties. Furthermore, both the Union Nationale and the Liberal Party went through leadership struggles that year. General elections could not be put off much longer. The armed forces and the police (along with the federal government) could only hope that a Liberal victory in Quebec would finally — and if possible, irreversibly — put all levels of government on the same wavelength.

Their wish came true as Robert Bourassa led his team to victory on April 29, 1970.

The following May 7, the federal cabinet created the special committee already mentioned to study the circumstances in which the War Measures Act might be proclaimed in the future. This decision (which did not become public knowledge until *The*

Globe and Mail published a secret cabinet document on December 23, 1971) was communicated only to a limited number of faithful allies of Pierre Trudeau.

At the same time, Jérôme Choquette, Quebec's new justice minister, drafted a bill on explosives intended primarily to give police extraordinary search and detention powers.

On May 27, 1970, the newspaper *La Presse* reported that planners in the Department of National Defence were giving "increasing attention to the question of civil disturbances in Canada." A veteran officer said in an Ottawa interview with the Canadian Press that he could not recall a period "when we paid more attention to the *role of the military in aid of the civil power.*" (Italics added) Nobody paid much attention to the article, however. *La Presse* also reported that under the National Defence Act, "the armed forces are required to comply with a request for assistance from a provincial attorney-general," and that they must await such a request before they can intervene. But at the time this procedural problem was being ironed out in talks with the Quebec justice department. *La Presse* added that the armed forces were in a "state of readiness" to respond to any request for intervention. The responsibility for the introduction of this state of readiness and for the execution of potential military operations had been entrusted to the Mobile Command headquarters in St. Hubert.*

In June and July, 1970, while commenting on recent FLQ bombings in Westmount and Ottawa, both Bourassa and Choquette stated that police knew who the terrorists were (which was true) and that only "ten to fifteen persons" belonged to the "fringe" group (which was also true).

A few months later, however, Choquette suddenly referred to a potential proclamation of the War Measures Act. On October 1 (four days before the Cross kidnapping), he announced that his

*La Presse, May 27, 1970

Explosives Control Act was coming into force that day after being passed by the Quebec National Assembly in July. He went on to comment that the legislation was based on provisions of the War Measures Act, which "in the 1939-45 period had given the RCMP powers similar" to those being granted, twenty-five years later, to the Quebec Police Force.*

How could the activities of a fringe group of "ten to fifteen persons" justify the passage of a special law on the control of explosives? How could such a group, already known to the police, also lead the authorities to consider the implementation of the War Measures Act? It was all the more surprising since, four months before the kidnappings of Cross and Laporte, Premier Bourassa had told reporters that "the police are on top of the matter."†

But as has already been argued, Operation Essay was not designed to crush the FLQ in October 1970, but to give the Québécois a lesson in toughness. The staging of this lesson required nonetheless the legislative and political co-operation of the Quebec government, which had the official responsibility of asking the federal government to proclaim the War Measures Act. Premier Robert Bourassa did this by signing on October 16, 1970, a letter drafted for him by Marc Lalonde.

During the crisis, co-ordination between Quebec and Ottawa was directed by Julien Chouinard, then the provincial executive secretary, and Marc Lalonde, who was Trudeau's principal political counsellor. Michel Côté represented the City of Montreal and later described himself as "the chief information man" (in a CBC interview), although in reality, the operation was managed from the Quebec Police headquarters in Montreal by the commanders of the 5th Combat Group and the officers of the Civil

---

* *The Montreal Star,* final edition, October 1, 1970
† Research material for the 1975 CBC documentary *The October Crisis,* unpublished.

Emergencies Section of the armed forces.

At any rate, the Cross kidnapping did not surprise Bourassa and Choquette, who were well aware from the start that the War Measures Act was about to be invoked — and with their full co-operation.

The "Agitators"

While the FLQ members found out that police had located all their operating quarters, including the house at 5630 Armstrong Street in St. Hubert, most of the Quebec *indépendantistes* floundered in defeatist attitudes following the April 29 election, when the Parti Québécois collected twenty-three per cent of the popular vote but won only seven seats.

Suddenly in September, this sullenness dissipated when an apparently well-founded rumour spread that a major offensive was being prepared. People were discussing this openly in Place Jacques Cartier bars in Old Montreal. What exactly was being prepared? "Something much more powerful than a bomb," it was said.

Many activists were thus alerted. Some believed that there was some truth to the accounts being circulated by a person who inspired confidence. Others remained skeptical because of the two kidnap plots that had aborted in the preceding months.

Through agents who had infiltrated practically everywhere, the police (especially the RCMP, which confirmed it later) happily seized on these rumours, exaggerating them for the benefit of certain politicians and by planting their own "decoy cells" inside the independence movement.* Among other things, it was hoped that these "cells" would convince the Parti Québécois executives in certain ridings to launch clandestine activities, or at least get them to publicly endorse the objectives

---

Ibid.

of the FLQ. Fortunately for the Parti Québécois, these tactics failed.

In any event, the *indépendantiste* circles of the left became agitated in September 1970. They knew nothing of the plans laid by the armed forces, the police and the federal government; in addition, they underrated Robert Bourassa as a "hopeless weakling". They felt they had to redeem the April 29 defeat. But how? They could not agree on any plan for action, but they unanimously hoped that there would be some action.

On October 5, the Cross kidnapping confirmed, with baffling ease and lack of security, the talk that had circulated for weeks. How could such a spectacular caper succeed when dozens of people spent the previous days predicting it to their friends? And when it was being discussed even in public?

Once the kidnappings had paved the way for the imposition of the War Measures Act, hundreds of arrests, the death of Pierre Laporte, the smashing of FRAP, the Montreal municipal coalition organized to oppose Jean Drapeau and his Civic Party, and eventually, the denunciation of the so-called "revolutionary parallel government," many *indépendantistes* recalled the rumours of September and began suspecting that the American intelligence agencies had played a role in those events.

Was the CIA Involved?

Like Canada as a whole, Quebec has become since the Second World War a virtual United States possession. For the multinational corporations as much as for the American government, Canada is expected to conform to a continental rationalization that not only involves control of military strategy, but political and economic control as well. The U.S. objective, in both the Northern and Southern Hemispheres, is to exercise direct control over the domestic and foreign markets of its satellites.

This hemispheric approach was spelled out clearly in a press conference by the then U.S. Secretary of State William Rogers on December 23, 1971, when he reaffirmed Washington's opposition to "secession movements" and the obligation for the U.S. to defend a nation's unity when a threat arises. Imperialist monopolies can make "indispensable changes" more easily in a unified territory than in a "balkanized" territory. It is with this in mind that in recent years the U.S. has selected Brazil as its "pre-eminent satellite" in the southern hemisphere; Bolivia, Paraguay and Uruguay have been annexed willy-nilly to Brazil, while Chile and Argentina have been brought to their knees. It is interesting to note that during the same period, Canada and Brazil improved their relations.

Ironically, a major step towards continental rationalization was being discussed privately at this time. On October 8, 1970, the fourth day of the crisis, Premier Robert Bourassa was in New York talking about "the role of major importance that Quebec can play in solving the problem of electric power shortages in the north-eastern states of the U.S." A few months later, once the crisis was over, he officially unveiled the James Bay hydro project, which involves major power exports to New York state. Both Bourassa and Trudeau have stressed the importance of foreign investment (primarily American) for this country's prosperity.

This objective of continental rationalization is presumably pursued by the CIA when it monitors the evolution of the overall situation in Canada and in Quebec.

Focussing on Quebec in particular, the Pentagon began a "Revolt Project" in 1962 that produced such interesting results that it served as the model for the "Camelot Project" aimed at Chile.*

---

* Debates of the House of Commons, February 26 to March 3, 1966. For details on Latin American studies, see *The Rise and Fall of Project Camelot*, M.I.T. Press, Cambridge, Mass., 1967

It is very well known that Canadian police forces maintain close links with the CIA and FBI. As for the Canadian military intelligence services, they are integrated with their counterparts in the U.S. and in "allied" countries in Europe.

So it would be quite naive to expect that in October 1970, the American intelligence agencies were content to observe from a distance the unfolding of Operation Essay and the federal attempt to eliminate the "separatist threat".

On September 24, 1971, *The Montreal Star* published a photocopy it had received of a very intriguing message from Washington dated October 20, 1970. The message read: "Subject: Quebec. Sources advise that urgent action be taken to temporarily break contacts with the FLQ militants since the Canadian government's measures may have undesirable consequences." Bearing the CIA letterhead and the initials R.D., the message suggested that the proclamation of the War Measures Act could disrupt the work of certain agents in Quebec.*

Despite the customary denials by the U.S. State Department, officials of the Canadian embassy in Washington told reporters that Ottawa took the matter "very seriously." But nothing more was heard about it.

Nothing further has been revealed about the nature of these "FLQ contacts". We can guess, however, on the basis of the military and police preparations mentioned above, that they likely played the role of agents provocateurs.

In any event, the information gathered by the RCMP, the Montreal police and various government agencies was automatically transmitted to Washington through the computer interconnections of several organizations, such as the Law Enforcement Intelligence Unit (LEIU).† This unit, a sort of Interpol specializing in anti-subversion operations, had compiled all the relevant

---

* *The Montreal Star,* September 24, 1971
† *The Montreal Star,* May 14, 1975

data on the FLQ when the October Crisis began. The LEIU is an American organization, divided into two huge administrative regions. The Western Region takes in the central and western states of the U.S. On the other hand, the Eastern Region comprises Canada's entire territory and the U.S. eastern seaboard. Needless to say, the Canadian Parliament has never been asked to approve the creation of this organization.

Members of the LEIU include senior officials of the Quebec Police Force and the Montreal Urban Community Police. Only high-ranking officers belonging to the organization (about 230 in all in the U.S. and Canada) have access to the LEIU data bank, which is called the Interstate Organized Crime Index and is located in an unmarked building owned by the California Justice Department. This data bank not only contains the identities and biographies of the leading organized crime figures, but also those of "radicals, dissidents, revolutionaries and persons of that sort."

It is therefore safe to assume that the armed forces, intelligence agencies and main police forces of the U.S. were aware in October 1970 of the projects of their Canadian and Quebec allies. It seems plausible that they would have been informed ahead of time about the expected kidnappings and the plans for Operation Essay. It is also possible that they participated directly in the preparation of Operation Essay.

During the court battle between dismissed RCMP officer Donald McCleery, who played a major role in the Cross kidnapping investigation, and his superiors, evidence was produced that at least two U.S. miliary intelligence agents in Montreal carried out certain missions and that the Pentagon's interest in the Quebec situation had been code-named RITA.* The McCleery

* Research material for the 1975 CBC documentary *The October Crisis*, unpublished.

case ended abruptly when these meagre disclosures emerged.*

For his part, Michel Côté revealed in research interviews for the 1975 CBC program on the October Crisis that "certain U.S. representatives" stayed at the Quebec Police headquarters (where the military officers were also located) for the duration of the crisis. Côté added that representatives of the British MI-5 were also present.** It seems that Washington was not the only foreign capital likely to have a "stake" in Operation Essay.

What about London?

After many years of entanglement in the Irish question, the British certainly had good reason to study the evolution of Operation Essay, whose lessons might one day prove useful to the experts at MI-5 and Scotland Yard.

James Cross himself received some training from MI-5.† Could it be that Cross was in fact an accomplice in his own kidnapping?

According to sources close to the former Bourassa cabinet, Cross had been forewarned by the authorities that he was in danger of being kidnapped and had agreed to serve as a volunteer hostage. Before accepting, however, he had demanded and received assurances that his life would not be endangered either by the eventual kidnappers or by law enforcement agencies. It was understood that his period of captivity would last about three weeks, four at the most. In fact, it lasted two months.

Again according to these sources, Susan Cross, the diplomat's daughter, had known several FLQ members since at least 1969,

---

* *The Toronto Star,* September 25, 1974

** Research material for the 1975 CBC documentary *The October Crisis,* unpublished.

† This was stated in October 1970 by FLQ lawyer Robert Lemieux and confirmed by British officials.

including Jacques Lanctôt and Paul Rose. She was reported to have visited La Maison du Pêcheur founded by the Rose brothers at Perçé during the summer of 1969, but she denied this in a 1972 interview with *Weekend* magazine. Did she serve as an intermediary in 1970? Some teachers in Lachute, where Susan Cross worked as a guidance counsellor in an English-language high school, have stated that they saw her in the company of Paul Rose before October 1970.* Montreal newspapers published reports along those lines during the crisis.

Susan Cross left Montreal secretly during the crisis, accompanying her mother to Berne, Switzerland. They left just before the opening of the coroner's inquest into the death of Pierre Laporte. Until the release of the diplomat, Mrs. Cross and her daughter stayed with the British ambassador's family in Berne. Why did they choose to stay in Switzerland instead of going back to Britain?

At any rate, on October 5, the Foreign Office issued a statement in London disclosing that the British trade commissioner in Montreal had just been kidnapped. This statement came one hour before the first special broadcast on the CBC French network. It attributed the kidnapping to the FLQ *two hours before* the FLQ claimed responsibility by planting four envelopes containing ransom notes at the Unversity of Quebec in Montreal.

According to Michel Côté, certain intelligence sections of the Canadian armed forces had British representatives in their ranks in 1970.

As it happens, the interview the CBC filmed with Côté was not used in the documentary *The October Crisis* broadcast in October 1975; nor was most of the information mentioned above about the military plans for domestic intervention. Several segments of the programs were deleted from the final version at the request of CBC management.

* Interviews by the author.

The unconditional support accorded to the Trudeau government in October 1970 by Washington and London appears to require no further explanation: Canada's two foremost allies had their own men on the scene — and they still do.

The Role of the Media

The secret preparations leading up to October 1970 still raise some questions about the role of the media. Were the managements of certain Montreal radio stations tipped off before the Cross kidnapping? Could it be that, during the early hours of the crisis, they were asked by the authorities to "pull out all the stops?" What we know for a fact is that the media needed very little time to mobilize their entire staffs for the coverage of "the events" and to concentrate the attention of the public on those events alone. A kidnapping that would probably have been seen elsewhere as one "exploit" of political militants among others quickly monopolized all attention in Quebec and continued to do so for months.

As was pointed out at the beginning of this chapter, this was precisely what the May 7 Committee wanted. The monopolization of public interest around "the crisis" was necessary to make the political shock treatment as effective as possible. It was necessary also that the capacity for cool analysis give way to sensationalism, overdramatization, public agitation and eventually collective fear. The whole population had to be swayed before the manipulation could work well. And what easier way to sway the public than to sway journalists and the electronic media? The effectiveness of this technique had been amply demonstrated by the infamous Brink's truck scare on the eve of the April 1970 election.

Consciously or not, the media played a leading role in the escalation of the October crisis. And curiously, until the death of

Pierre Laporte (which marked the end of the political phase of the crisis, as we shall see in the next chapter), the police and the political authorities showed a remarkable tolerance toward the exploitation of the FLQ actions by the media. This tolerance and "freedom of information" was such that, after the Laporte kidnapping, Justice Minister Choquette rejected offers from certain newsmen to help police track down the FLQ members, or at least their messengers.* Some of the newsmen involved concluded that the police did not really need them in order to be well informed and that the police were giving free rein to the FLQ kidnappers while watching them closely.

The tolerance of the authorities ended abruptly on October 17, 1970. That morning, Choquette convened an "off-the-record briefing" (his own expression), attended by about seventy-five representatives of the media, to urge them to follow "a tighter discipline." That same evening the body of Pierre Laporte was found, not by the police, but by reporters from radio station CKAC. About the same time, the Quebec Police director barred journalists from the press room that had been set up in previous days at his headquarters. And on October 15, CBC president George Davidson instructed the staff of the publicly owned corporation to avoid all speculation while covering the event *in future.*

Davidson's instructions resulted from confidential moves by Gérard Pelletier, then the minister responsible for the CBC. On the afternoon of October 15, the minister had unusual telephone conversations with executives of Canada's most influential electronic media — the CBC and CTV networks and the Canadian Press wire service, which also operates a radio news service. Pelletier told the executives that the "next forty-eight hours" would be a crucial period in the crisis (early the following

* Research material for the 1975 CBC documentary *The October Crisis*, unpublished.

morning the War Measures Act was proclaimed and the next day Laporte was killed). He stressed that it was important that news media stop spreading "unconfirmed rumours" and "speculation" about impending developments (which did not stop the CBC from erroneously reporting the death of James Cross on the night of October 17). Besides Davidson, the minister spoke to Tom Gould, vice-president of CTV for news and public affairs, and John Dauphinee, general manager of Canadian Press.*

Certainly, before October 16, the media were allowed to "exceed the limits of public interest" (as Davidson put it in an interview) without any restrictions. After that date, which coincided with the imposition of the War Measures Act, the media were told to submit to the "tight discipline" of censorship and self-censorship.

Without questioning their actions very much, the media played the part that had been "allocated in advance"† to them by the federal authorities. First, focus the full attention of the people of Quebec on the "FLQ exploits"; then in the second phase, once tension had reached fever pitch, transmit the decisive shock into every home — the imposition of War Measures and, the next day, the "execution" of Pierre Laporte. Once this had been done, and done well, it became child's play for the authorities to sell the official version of the crisis.

Besides, after working around the clock for two weeks, journalists were numb with exhaustion, absolutely flat. The restoration of "discipline" in the media gave them a well-earned rest.

After that point, the political and psychological manipulation of the public reached such intensity that the journalists were unable to recover their senses until the storm blew itself out.

---

* These facts were revealed by Tom Gould and several CBC executives in interviews with CBC researchers in 1975, but the material was omitted from the documentary *The October Crisis*.

† Gérard Pelletier, *op. cit.*, pp. 127-131

2

OPERATION ESSAY UNFOLDS

I wonder if any Canadian government besides the one led by Pierre Trudeau would have dared — in order to thwart the Quebec independence movement — to assume so callously the responsibility for unleashing and carrying out Operation Essay.

This kind of "political courage" can only be explained by a fierce determination to slay the nationalism that, since 1960, has been the catalyst for the advocacy of sovereignty and independence for a people condemned to assimilation in 1838 by Lord Durham.

As Louis Martin wrote in 1975; for Pierre Trudeau, Jean Marchand, Marc Lalonde, Gérard Pelletier, Jean-Pierre Goyer and company, "the nationalist ideal in Quebec amounts to a permanent conspiracy against democracy. The notion of a provisional government, to prop up the Bourassa cabinet, was not born with the October crisis; in Trudeau's mind, it was born with Québécois nationalism, which the prime minister has always dreamed of *annihilating*."*

Five months after the 1970 election in Quebec, therefore, the time seemed ripe for the federal authorities to deal a death blow to the *indépendantistes'* hopes by entrapping them in a

---

*Louis Martin, "Le vrai complot" ("The Real Plot"), *Le Magazine Maclean*, November 1975.

pseudo-plot against democracy. What follows is a day-to-day chronicle of the events of the crisis.

October 5

About 8:30 a.m., British diplomat James Cross is kidnapped at his residence by the Liberation Cell of the Front de Libération du Québec.

In the record time of two hours, 3,000 circulars bearing a photograph and description of Cross are distributed to all police stations and the media. This operation is carried out so quickly that some reporters have the impression the circulars were printed before the kidnapping.* A few days later, Michel Auger was to report in *La Presse* that another circular, this time confidential, coming from the anti-terrorist squad and bearing pictures of five suspects in the Cross kidnapping, was not printed on the same kind of paper as was normally used for such circulars and did not carry the name of any police force. Auger added: "This circular has not received very wide distribution."**

Two hours after the diplomat's kidnapping, *La Presse* publishes a story by Jean de Guise forecasting that the FLQ's demands probably will be the same ones that were listed in the manifesto seized by police the previous June. De Guise also makes a connection between that day's kidnapping and Jacques Lanctôt, who had been arrested in February 1970 in connection with another kidnap plot and whose brother François had been arrested in connection with the June plot.† His deductions are accurate, but police spokesmen nonetheless claim that the case is a complete mystery.

* Unpublished material prepared for the 1975 CBC documentary *The October Crisis*.
** *La Presse,* October 13, 1970
† *La Presse,* October 5, 1970

Early in the afternoon, Justice Minister Jérôme Choquette calls a press conference after conferring with representatives of the RCMP, the QPF and the CAT squad. He announces that Cross's life is in danger because the diplomat suffers from high blood pressure. The suspense begins.

At the same time, Colette Duhaime, a reporter with *Le Journal de Montreal,* is approached by a self-styled FLQ activist arrested and released earlier in 1970, who asks if she would like to interview . . . James Cross! Sensing that the man is a police informer who may be trying to implicate her, she dismisses him.

October 6

At 9:30 a.m., radio and TV stations read the contents of the first communiqués from the Liberation Cell, picked up by police the previous day at the University of Quebec in Montreal. *La Presse* comes out with a front-page banner proclaiming, "Bourassa, Trudeau and Drapeau are on the list of FLQ targets." The suspense grows more intense. At 6:00 p.m., a communiqué from the Liberation Cell warns that Cross runs the risk of being executed if the powers that be do not show flexibility.

Through the day, Prime Minister Trudeau presides over a meeting of the cabinet committee on priorities. A key decision emerges from the long session — the government will not negotiate over the FLQ demands but will *pretend* to be willing to do so in an effort to buy time. Premier Bourassa endorses this strategy. (A special telephone line is installed to link Trudeau and Bourassa directly and minimize the possibility of leaks.) At 8:00 p.m., External Affairs Minister Mitchell Sharp says in a prepared statement read in the House of Commons that "these are wholly unreasonable demands and their authors could not have expected them to be accepted." At the same time, he hints at negotiations by urging the Cross kidnappers to name a spokesman.*

October 7

Pierre Trudeau reiterates at 9:30 a.m. his government's refusal to accede to the FLQ demands. At 1:00 p.m., Mrs. Cross identifies Jacques Lanctôt as one of her husband's kidnappers while examining pictures from police files.

Meanwhile, Mobile Command calls Quebec Police Director Maurice St. Pierre. The armed forces representative expresses some impatience. The QPF director explains that it is too early to call in troops, but he turns over to Mobile Command a map which he says police found in a recent raid. The map shows the layout of Depot 34 at Camp Bouchard at Ste. Thérèse, where large quantities of munitions are stored.

St. Pierre and Mobile Command finally agree that the troops can begin moving to "protect" Camp Bouchard. During the night, elements of the 12th Armoured Regiment leave Valcartier to take up positions at Ste. Thérèse, fifteen miles north of Montreal.†

At 11:30 p.m., radio station CKAC broadcasts the full text of the FLQ manifesto, copies of which are obtained by at least two Montreal dailies as well.

It is around this time that the Rose brothers, their mother and Francis Simard return to Montreal from a mysterious trip to Texas.

---

* Details of the government's secret strategy were reported by Walter Stewart in
  Shrug: Trudeau in Power, new press, 1972, p. 55.
† CBC, *Background to Military Role,* p. 12

October 8

The Montreal Stock Exchange seals off its visitors' gallery because officials fear a bombing.

During the afternoon, the CBC broadcasts an unfounded rumor that James Cross has been murdered. The false report spreads immediately to the federal Parliament, where Mitchell Sharp is seen coming and going in haste. Members of Parliament react with anguish.

An armed forces spokesman assures reporters that the troop movements seen around Camp Bouchard have absolutely no connection with the new situation in Quebec. The Quebec Police Force issues a similar denial. Journalists agree that it would be ridiculous to mobilize the armed forces over a single kidnapping.

At 10:30 p.m., the French television network of the CBC broadcasts the FLQ manifesto, "for humanitarian reasons." Thousands of Québécois cheer the accusing statement. On the other hand, Marcel Masse, former member of the Johnson cabinet, comments that the manifesto leaves him "puzzled", since "Quebec's demands go *much further* than that."*

In fact, the FLQ manifesto was aimed primarily at making the Quebec situation known to world opinion. It also emphasized that the FLQ was not attempting to bring about a coup d'état, but simply to win the release of the political prisoners while scoring a propaganda victory. In this context, the Cross kidnapping was intended as an act of "armed propaganda" and not the beginning of a war of attrition against the existing system. A communiqué dated October 27 was to repeat this theme, but the police forbade its publication at that time.

In his column in *Le Journal de Montréal,* René Lévesque denounces "the hypocrisy of the official circles" and, that

---

* Jacques Lacoursière, *Alarme Citoyens,* Editions La Presse, 1972, pp. 126-7.

evening, he angrily condemns those who attempt to link the Cross kidnapping with the Parti Québécois.

A short time later, a member of the Trudeau cabinet tells a CBC reporter privately that the crisis will "kill" Lévesque politically, because the jousting match between the FLQ and the government "is too rough for him."

October 9

At 12:15 a.m., radio stations report that the armed forces have been placed on alert.

Mobile Command is checking the disposition of troops all across Canada. But the Quebec Police director feels it is still too soon for a military occupation of Quebec.

The Strategic Operations Centre, located at 67 Sparks Street in Ottawa, buzzes with activity twenty-four hours a day, as does the East Block "war room" located near the prime minister's office.

Rumours about an eventual proclamation of the War Measures Act begin circulating in the federal capital.

October 10

Prime Minister Trudeau is scheduled to announce his government's definitive position at 3:00 p.m., but his press conference is cancelled. Instead, Quebec Justice Minister Jérôme Choquette goes on television at 5:40 p.m. to read the *final* decision of the authorities.

This decision is a categorical refusal to release the political prisoners. But the refusal is coupled with an offer to provide safe conduct to a foreign country for the kidnappers of James Cross.

A few minutes later, at 6:18 p.m., Pierre Laporte, the political strongman of the Bourassa cabinet, acting premier and minister of labour and immigration, is abducted in front of his home.

General stupefaction. Those who had doubts about the FLQ's strength must now resign themselves to the fact that "the revolutionary threat" is for real. Many people begin to panic.

Flabbergasted by this daring blow, the Liberation Cell members cannot hide their surprise from James Cross. Events are taking an abrupt turn that they had not expected. The kidnapping of Pierre Laporte has just robbed them of the initiative in the field of armed propaganda.

As in the Cross kidnapping, the police answer the call by rushing to the wrong house, that of one of the Laporte family's neighbours. Laporte's kidnappers vanish in a matter of seconds like Cross' kidnappers before them, but some witnesses take down their license number. No one can understand how it could happen — as is noted in the next chapter, the neighbourhood where the Laporte family lives has been patrolled regularly by the police.

Once again, police say that they have been caught completely off guard by the FLQ, which will not send out its first communiqué until the next morning.

At 10:00 p.m., the CBC French network reports it has received an anonymous telephone call warning that "Pierre Laporte will be liquidated" if the authorities do not comply with all the demands of the FLQ.

The dramatization of the crisis triggered on October 5 has now reached the point of no return. The FLQ cannot aim any higher now, unless it kidnaps Premier Bourassa himself.

The premier had returned to Quebec a few hours before the Laporte kidnapping and joined his family in Sorel. He had cancelled a scheduled meeting with Senator Edward Kennedy in Boston. The premier's plane had been unable to land at the Boston airport because of fog.

October 11

After meeting the justice minister during the night, Bourassa decides to move into the Queen Elizabeth Hotel with his entire cabinet.

Robert Lemieux, the lawyer, is arrested and held in custody on a charge of interfering in the police investigation through his media interviews. His files are seized. The Quebec Police director takes part in the first special meeting of the Bourassa cabinet. Maurice St. Pierre now calls for the armed forces' intervention. He says his request is justified for the following reasons: 1) his men are exhausted; 2) a large number of policemen are tied up as bodyguards for public figures; 3) the arrival of troops in Ottawa is imminent; 4) it is important for the Quebec Police to question hundreds of "suspects" to flesh out the files of the anti-subversive squad, which requires that as many policemen as possible be freed for the interrogations.

Certain members of the cabinet hesitate to grant St. Pierre's wishes. But the QPF director notifies the armed forces that he has formally recommended their intervention. Ottawa is immediately informed.

For his part, Mayor Jean Drapeau states that the situation is critical and that Canadian unity is directly threatened.

A short time later, CKAC broadcasts the contents of Pierre Laporte's extremely pathetic letter to Bourassa (see Appendix III). "Decide whether I will live or die," the minister writes, stressing the urgency of the situation.

At 9:55 p.m., in a brief televised statement, Bourassa replies: "To govern is to choose."

After discussions between Mobile Command and Quebec Police headquarters, it is decided that the troops will enter Montreal at 1:00 p.m. on October 14. Even though the Bourassa cabinet still cannot agree on the armed forces' intervention, the

Civil Emergencies Section of Mobile Command moves into the QPF headquarters on Parthenais Street in Montreal.*

October 12

Members of the Parti Québécois executive hold an emergency meeting. Some 500 troops move into Ottawa. Laporte's kidnappers warn in a communiqué that even if the authorities free the political prisoners (which had been the main demand of the Cross kidnappers) "the minister for the unemployment and the assimilation of the Québécois will not be released."

The 2nd and 3rd Battalions of the Royal 22nd Regiment are placed on alert at Valcartier while awaiting the official request for intervention from the Quebec government.

Just before midnight, Premier Bourassa's office announces the establishment of "machinery for negotiations." The more liberal members of the cabinet can sigh with relief. The decision to open "negotiations" has been made jointly by Quebec and Ottawa to "gain time".

Lawyers Robert Demers and Robert Lemieux will act as negotiators, the former for the Quebec government, the latter for the FLQ. Demers represents the provincial government, but most of the FLQ demands can only be met by the federal government.

Late at night, Mobile Command sends an emissary to hand over to Justice Minister Choquette the official letter he has to sign to request, on behalf of the Quebec government, the intervention of the armed forces. Choquette emerges fuming from a cabinet meeting; he still has not obtained the necessary approval. Plans for a military intervention on October 14 have to be postponed for twenty-four hours.†

Growing increasingly exasperated with the "soft attitude" of

*CBC, *op. cit.*, p. 19
†*Ibid.*, p. 18

some of his colleagues, Choquette asks the federal cabinet to help him convince the refractory Quebec ministers.*

October 13

The "negotiations" begin in complete ambiguity. Lemieux rejects the first proposal from Bourassa's emissary. At 6:15 p.m. Lemieux tells reporters that "the negotiations have virtually broken down."

The Bourassa government replies that "a preliminary question must be settled" before negotiations can begin on the FLQ demands, meaning that the FLQ must guarantee the safe return of the hostages.

(On October 11, the premier's executive assistant, Guy Langlois, had led associates of Pierre Laporte to believe that the Bourassa government was ready to "accept all the FLQ demands in order to save his life.")

The pretence of negotiating will continue in this way until October 15.

October 14

Members of the Bourassa cabinet finally agree to back the hard line.

The police keep Paul Rose under surveillance without interfering with his movements. (Solicitor-General McIlraith will confirm this on November 2 in the Commons.)

Communications specialists from the Canadian armed forces set up facilities next to the premier's office in the Quebec Assembly.

The proclamation of the War Measures Act is scheduled for October 16 at 4:00 a.m.†

Ibid., p. 19
† *Ibid.*

The Quebec Police Force completes the list of the hundreds of people it plans to arrest in the first big sweep.

October 15

The people of Quebec are extremely tense.

At 7:00 a.m., St. Pierre orders the closing of the press room set up earlier in the crisis at QPF headquarters.

Troop movements begin gingerly, while an army officer finally obtains a duly signed request for military intervention from Justice Minister Choquette. The letter is rushed to Ottawa by air to avoid delays in the deployment of armed forces units.

The Quebec request, as expected, is accepted immediately. Mobile Command gets the green light.

Meanwhile, the Bourassa government appoints Maurice St. Pierre as director of all local police forces in Quebec. The appointment is made through a simple order-in-council (No. 3772), effective immediately.

About 2:00 p.m., troops in battle gear begin arriving by air at the St. Hubert base, some of them from as far away as Edmonton. General Michael Dare has given the order for the beginning of Operation Essay across the country. From the Northwest Territories to Newfoundland, exercises have been planned to test the effectiveness of the armed forces' logistics. By evening, all military units in the country have taken up their assigned positions and policemen are ordered to report to their detachments.

In the Montreal region, guard duty is assigned to the 2nd and 3rd Battalions of the Royal 22nd Regiment.

The command post of the 5th Combat Group at Quebec Police headquarters handles the co-ordination of Operation Essay in Quebec.* Under the National Defence Act, the troops theoretically come under the authority of the Quebec Police director.

Ibid., p. 26

At 9:00 a.m., Premier Bourassa rejects the FLQ demands, offers the Cross and Laporte kidnappers safe conduct to a foreign country and gives them a *final* deadline of six hours to respond.

Montreal Police Chief Marcel St. Aubin, the Montreal municipal authorities and Premier Bourassa send official requests for assistance to Ottawa. Montreal calls for increased federal aid, without specifying which kind, while Quebec clearly asks Ottawa to proclaim the War Measures Act. The Quebec request was drafted largely by Marc Lalonde and Bourassa's chief contribution was to sign it. (This fact was revealed on October 23, 1973 by Claude Morin, who was Quebec's deputy minister of intergovernmental affairs in 1970.)

The pseudo-negotiations between the authorities and the FLQ are obviously off.

Radio and television commentators express deep concern over the turn of events. A growing fear grips the public. Unable to sleep, many people stay up all night.

October 16

At 4:00 a.m., the Governor-General in Council approves an emergency proclamation that automatically brings the War Measures Act into force. Instantly, a roundup of hundreds of Québécois begins, without arrest warrants.

As the House of Commons opens debate on a government motion endorsing the War Measures Act, Jean Marchand suggests that without such an extreme step, Quebec would have separated within a year. In a television address, Trudeau brands FLQ members as "assassins". In Quebec, Premier Bourassa tells reporters he recommended the imposition of War Measures because he feared "selective assassinations" of public figures. Mayor Drapeau issues a statement claiming that urgent action was needed to foil "a four-stage plan" to overthrow the government. Despite all the official references to an "apprehended insurrection", calm prevails in every part of Quebec.

Members of the Liberation Cell holding Cross decide to write a commmuniqué urging the press to denounce the "coup" perpetrated by the federal authorities. Publication of this message is banned by the police under the terms of the War Measures Act.

The ping-pong game between the FLQ and the authorities is definitely over. Now the time has come for Ottawa to demonstrate to the people that "this is war."

René Lévesque suspects that the crisis has been fabricated by those in power. He says in a statement: "We cannot help thinking and saying that this degradation of Quebec was intended, quite deliberately." He also points out that "the half-government we had until now has been swept away by the first hard blow." Referring to the massive manhunts under way throughout Quebec since the early hours of the morning, he adds that the Québécois are witnessing an operation aimed solely at "disorganizing and dislocating, or at least trying to compromise and demoralize *as much as possible,* most of the groups and organizations that give a democratic expression to the Québécois' *most legitimate aspirations and collective needs.*" The Parti Québécois leader concludes that this operation dangerously compromises "all our chances for a future."

In his own statement, Pierre Trudeau lumps the protection of "fundamental rights" with the defence of national unity. He states that his government has an obligation to defend the state against "insurrection".

October 17

A communiqué from a so-called Dieppe (Royal 22nd) Cell announces that Pierre Laporte has been "executed". His body is found on federal territory at the St. Hubert airport, a few hundred yards from the armed forces' Mobile Command headquarters.

The terrorization of the Québécois people is now disguised as a gigantic manhunt.

Now that the mass political shock treatment has reached its peak intensity, the federal government can get the desired response. In a poll taken a few days later, eighty-five per cent of the Québécois respondents will approve the proclamation of the War Measures Act, which the federal government will interpret as an unequivocal rejection of the independence cause.

Politically, the crisis is a complete success . . . for the federal authorities.

Trudeau, Bourassa and the media all suggest that the fugitive members of the Chénier Cell of the FLQ are the murderers of the minister.

It will take *three weeks* for the pathologists to publish their final autopsy report, three weeks for the Quebec justice department to order an inquest and appoint the presiding coroner, and three weeks for police to arrest the first potential murder suspect, Bernard Lortie.

From October 18 to November 5

Pierre Laporte's death gives rise to all sorts of conflicting rumours. These rumours are fanned by the police and disseminated by the media. Many people, including Mayor Drapeau, claim openly that the minister was tortured. One radio station even reports that he was left to "bleed to death."

On October 21, after the minister's funeral, the Quebec government finally scotches these rumours by issuing a preliminary autopsy report signed by Dr. Jean-Paul Valcourt and Dr. Jean Hould. According to this report, Laporte was strangled with the flimsy religious medal chain he wore around his neck. As for the other wounds on the body, they are dismissed as "rather superficial cuts and scratches."

Warrants for the arrests of Paul Rose and Marc Carbonneau are transmitted to police forces across the country.

The federal authorities start a rumour about an alleged plot to stage a separatist coup d'état in Quebec involving leaders of the three labor federations, the Parti Québécois and the newspaper *Le Devoir*.

On October 25, Jean Drapeau wins re-election as mayor of Montreal with ninety-two per cent of the votes. He had accused his election opponents of having Laporte's blood on their hands. Jacques Parizeau states on October 26 that Ottawa seized on the kidnappings to begin its inevitable confrontation with Quebec.

On October 27, an FLQ communiqué attributed later to Paul Rose refers to the Dieppe raid, when Québécois troops "were *forced* to serve as guinea pigs." The same day, another communiqué signed "Dieppe Royal 22nd" claims that James Cross has been killed.

Robert Bourassa says in a prepared statement that he had been informed there was a possibility that a sort of provisional government might be formed in Quebec. Mayor Drapeau does likewise, talking about "the formation of a provisional government that would have been a collection of revolutionaries."

The next day, October 28, Pierre Trudeau identifies Claude Ryan, editor-publisher of *Le Devoir,* as the instigator of the plot.

On October 30, the Parti Québécois calls for a public inquiry into the causes and circumstances of the crisis. (On October 15, the PQ members of the Quebec National Assembly had tabled a motion for an emergency debate on "the problem concerning the safety of the member for Chambly," Pierre Laporte. The Bourassa government had opposed the motion in the name of "national security".)

Also on October 30, a group of Laporte's friends charges in a letter to *Le Devoir* that the authorities had set out "day by day and hour by hour . . . the horrible fate" of the minister. They add: "We would have every reason to be revengeful. But if we were, there would always be plenty of time for that."

On November 2, federal Justice Minister John Turner introduces the Public Order Temporary Measures Act, largely based on the War Measures Act (see Appendix II). This so-called Turner Act is to expire on April 30, 1971, even though Trudeau and Bourassa would have preferred to extend it indefinitely.

On November 5, twenty-four of the individuals interned since October 16 file into the coroner's court at the Quebec Police headquarters. They are charged with engaging in a "seditious conspiracy" or belonging to an illegal organization, namely the FLQ.

November 6

This is a great day for coincidences:

The pathologists, Dr. Valcourt and Dr. Hould, complete their final autopsy report, twenty days after Laporte's death.

The Quebec justice department names Judge Jacques Trahan as special coroner in the Laporte case.

Bernard Lortie and three other youths are arrested in a raid at an apartment on Queen Mary Road, near the University of Montreal campus.

RCMP Commissioner W.L. Higgitt predicts in an interview that the FLQ will crumble like a house of cards in a matter of hours.

The crisis has been under way for one month.

From November 7 to December 3

The coroner's inquest opens on November 7 at the Quebec Police headquarters. Judge Trahan states that he wants to conduct the inquest "expeditiously". His hearings will raise more questions than they will answer convincingly about the motives and circumstances behind the kidnapping and slaying of Pierre Laporte.

On November 12, Robert Bourassa declares that he favors "a re-examination of the manner in which freedom has been exercised and of the inherent dangers of verbal violence."

A Liberal member of the Quebec Assembly, Jean Bienvenue, in an outspoken speech on November 17, advocates "virile censorship" of films, books and magazines and "a purge if necessary" in the newsrooms of the press and broadcasting stations.

On November 26, newspapers report for the first time that many policemen are grumbling about interference in their work by senior officers and politicians. Later, word will leak out that some Québécois servicemen defied orders from their superiors, which slowed down the pace of Operation Essay. These "separatists" will be expelled from the armed forces in 1971.

On December 1, after a long opposition filibuster, the Turner Act is finally passed by the House of Commons, by a vote of 174 to 31. The next day, the bill is passed by the Senate and on December 3, it receives Royal Assent. The same day, by a "pure coincidence," James Cross is set free and his kidnappers are exiled to Cuba.

The crisis has been under way for two months.

From December 4 to 28

On December 8, Detective-Sergeant Gaston Roussin, president of the Montreal North Police Brotherhood, states that "the Cross-Laporte case is no longer a police investigation, but a political springboard." He compares the military deployment that surrounded the release of James Cross to "a Santa Claus parade."

On December 17, police and troops mount a massive operation in the south shore suburb of Longueuil, setting up road-blocks and conducting house-to-house searches.

On December 22, special prosecutor Yves Fortier requests that the coroner's inquest be adjourned to January 4, which is done. The next day, by coincidence, Prime Minister Trudeau announces that the armed forces will complete their withdrawal from Quebec on January 4.

In the early hours of December 28, Paul Rose, Jacques Rose and Francis Simard are arrested in a farmhouse at St. Luc. On January 4, they will appear at the inquest and Judge Trahan will find them "criminally responsible" for the death of Pierre Laporte. The next day, they will be arraigned on murder and kidnapping charges.

This occurs on January 5, 1971, three months to the day after the James Cross kidnapping.

Separatism Goes on Trial

Paul Rose's murder trial, billed as "the trial of the century" by Montreal newspapers, began on January 25, 1971. Four days later, Justice Marcel Nichols found Rose in contempt and expelled him from the courtroom for the day after the accused charged that the judge was in collusion with the Crown prosecutor. A series of similar expulsions followed in the next few days and on February 8, Rose was excluded from his trial for the remainder of the presentation of Crown evidence. In his address to the jury on March 12, he admitted being an FLQ member and said he and his friends were "proud of the actions we have taken," but he rejected the unsigned "confession" as a police fabrication. Rose implied that he had participated in the kidnapping of Laporte but not in his slaying. "If we do not talk about the death of Pierre Laporte, it is because of solidarity, a question of solidarity that affects all FLQ members," he said. At another point he stated that there were only twenty individuals in the 1970 version of the FLQ. The Rose trial, which ended on March 13 with a murder conviction and a life sentence, failed to shed any light on the real circumstances of Laporte's death. At the later trials, the other accused repudiated their alleged confessions and no new facts emerged.

Beyond these scapegoats, the whole independence movement was being placed on trial by the authorities. In May 1964, well before the founding of the Parti Québécois, Pierre Trudeau had equated this movement with criminal violence in a *Cité Libre* article.* Trudeau wrote then about the Québécois *indépendantistes*: "And when things don't go fast enough, they resort to lawlessness and violence." These comments were repeated in 1968, when Jacques Hébert collected Trudeau's articles and published them in book form on the eve of the Liberal leadership convention that chose Trudeau.

In 1970, one of the purposes of Operation Essay was to equate Quebec separatism with terror. Three months to the day after the Cross kidnapping, the arraignment of Laporte's alleged assassins was supposed to convince the public firmly that Trudeau's political views were well founded; more specifically, that "the separatists" were ready to resort even to murder to separate Quebec from Canada.

A death did indeed occur; but the question that remains unanswered is who was in fact responsible for it.

The War Measures Act gave the Trudeau government the legal powers to "choose between the life and death", not only of one man, but of a nation as well, or at least of the asprirations for

---

* Pierre Trudeau, "Les separatistes: des contre-revolutionnaires", *Cité Libre*, May 1964.

independence that were growing within that nation.*

The "apprehended insurrection" of October 1970 had existed since 1960 . . . and it has had more vigour than ever since November 15, 1976. This insurrection is the rise of the independence movement, which Trudeau compared in 1964, in all seriousness, to the rise of Hitler's fascism in the thirties.

As for the War Measures Act, whose abolition was promised after the events of 1970, it is still being held in reserve in the federal political arsenal. In this sense, as Ron Haggart and Aubrey Golden wrote in their book on the crisis, *Rumours of War,* Canada became "a changed nation" under Trudeau.** It is no longer that democracy whose liberalism formerly won praise in Western capitals. "There is only one kind of country in which people go to jail without suspicion of crime," where preventive internment serves to crush legal "opposition to government policies", and where "a combined package of police powers" makes it possible, at any time, to terrorize a whole population — a dictatorship.†

By its very existence, the War Measures Act makes Canada a unique democracy in the West. The act can be invoked in peacetime as soon as the key words "apprehended insurrection" are used by the cabinet. Canada is the only democracy that grants its elected leaders, "in case of need," all the powers of an absolute monarchy.

It must be conceded, however, that if Pierre Laporte had not been "executed" on October 17, 1970, the Trudeau government would have been hard put to justify invoking the War Measures. On October 16, this decision was strongly opposed in Parliament and David Lewis called it "excessive, hysterical and unacceptable."

* Ron Haggart and Aubrey Golden, *Rumours of War,* new press, 1971, p. 253-4.
** *Ibid.,* p. 267
† *Ibid.,* p. 249-74

Six years later, unfortunately, the Canadian Parliament has yet to repeal the War Measures Act or at least to prohibit its imposition in peacetime, apparently preferring the risks of an abuse of power to those of "separatism".

The Laporte house at the corner of Robitaille and Berkley in St. Lambert. Pierre Laporte was picked up by kidnappers when he stepped outside the house, in full view of his nephew, several neighbours and his wife.

An aerial photo of the Laporte house. The letters CL at the bottom of the photo were written in by police, and indicate where Pierre Laporte's nephew Claude Laporte was standing at the time of the kidnapping.

The house on Armstrong Street, where Laporte was allegedly held. The debris at the front of the house was left after the police raid which followed the discovery of Laporte's body.

The rear of the Armstrong Street house.

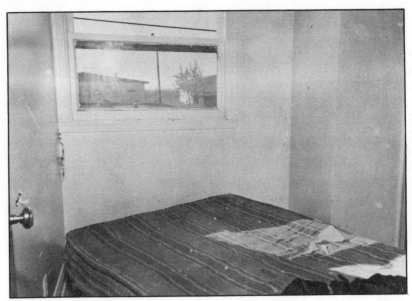

Inside the rear bedroom of the Armstrong Street house.

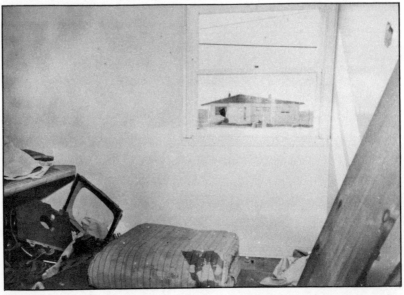

The same rear bedroom window. It was through the top of this window that Laporte allegedly jumped in an attempt to escape. This photo was taken by police, after their raid on the house. Note the smashed TV set.

The living room of the Armstrong Street house, showing the mess caused by police in the raid. Initials on the photo are police markings.

Michel Viger's rented farmhouse at St. Luc where the Rose brothers and Francis Simard were arrested by police.

The tunnel beneath the basement floor in the St. Luc farmhouse where Simard and the Rose brothers hid.

Pierre Laporte's religious medal and chain. The chain, tested for strength only after police investigations of the kidnapping were complete, was allegedly used to strangle Laporte.

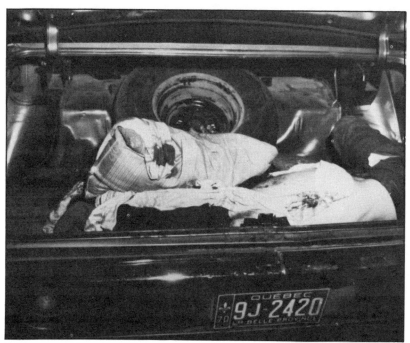

A close-up of Laporte's body in the trunk of the Chevrolet, found on federal territory at St. Hubert airport by a radio station reporter.

3

THE ASSASSINATION

Less than twenty-four hours after his October 10 kidnapping, Pierre Laporte wrote in a pathetic letter to Premier Bourassa: "Decide whether I will live or die."

"Laporte caught on fast," observes the prominent Quebec novelist Jacques Ferron, who was a friend of Laporte's. "He realized that he had been abandoned." He certainly must have realized that he had been sacrificed for reasons of state when he heard Bourassa declare on television on October 11, 1970, that "in a rare demonstration of its cruelty, fate determined that the preservation of public order must rest on him."

It was precisely a set of "Regulations to Provide Emergency Powers for the Preservation of Public Order in Canada" that Parliament was asked "as a formality," to debate on October 16.

And the next day, as if to demonstrate the need for such War Measures Act regulations, news media around the world reported the "execution" of Pierre Laporte.

Until Laporte's death was announced officially, the debate in the House of Commons revealed a wide disagreement between the Trudeau cabinet and the leading Opposition spokesmen over the imposition of the War Measures Act in peacetime and the suspension in practice of civil and constitutional rights in Canada, and more particularly in Quebec.

The previous Thursday, October 15, at 10:30 p.m., Prime

Minister Trudeau had tried vainly, in a private meeting, to win the support of Robert Stanfield and T.C. Douglas for his decision to proclaim a "state of war." Everything was ready at the cabinet level — the public order regulations and the list of persons to be interned under those regulations.

The same evening at 9:00 p.m., Robert Bourassa had "given" the FLQ a final deadline of six hours. The premier's letter (drafted by Marc Lalonde) urging the invocation of the War Measures Act conveniently reached Ottawa at 3:00 a.m. the next morning.*

One hour later, the "state of war" became official.

On Friday, October 16, therefore, the Opposition was confronted with a fait accompli. Opposition members did not know how the War Measures Act would be enforced exactly; they were in a poor position to make judgments, since the "relevant facts" remained secret, and they were being stampeded by a flurry of alarming rumours and notes that the Trudeau cabinet spread in the Commons lobbies.

Despite all this, the Opposition intended to resist the "wind of madness temporarily sweeping across Canada."† Stanfield and Douglas indicated that they would vote against the fait accompli.

On Saturday, a groundswell of opposition to the War Measures Act gained unexpected strength. But, after midnight, the spirited debate in the Commons was suddenly interrupted by the news of Laporte's slaying. The CBC even reported that James Cross was believed dead, too.

Immediately, the Opposition's attitude was likened to treason.

* In an interview with *Le Devoir* published September 18, 1976, Marc Lalonde commented: "I am a man who likes things to be well managed, to be clear and simple." In October 1970 he was in charge of the "legal" enforcement of the War Measures Act in Quebec.

† The day of the James Cross kidnapping, Pierre Laporte played down the abduction as a "wind of madness temporarily sweeping across Canada which will die down." See Jacques Lacoursière, *Alarme Citoyens*, p. 177.

Trudeau's position was completely vindicated.

At last, the ''French Power'' team could, with the support of the whole country, put Quebec in its place and deal a lethal blow to dreams of independence.*

In the general outrage, Trudeau had no trouble getting the majority of the people to believe that he was right when he imposed the War Measures because Laporte had been murdered.

From then on, FLQ members were branded as cold-blooded murderers and barbarians; the hundreds of Québécois who had already been interned or subjected to searches were suspected of participation in a dark and blood-thirsty plot to overthrow the established order; the army of ''3,000 FLQ terrorists'' mentioned by Jean Marchand became an accepted fact; some members of the Parti Québécois thought they would be driven underground like the early Christians in the Catacombs.

The FLQ as Absolute Evil

The FLQ manifesto had aroused widespread sympathy among the people of Quebec by denouncing social injustices in spectacular terms. But the announcement of Laporte's ''execution'' by a mysterious Dieppe (Royal 22nd) Cell destroyed this sympathy overnight and replaced it with a massive wave of indignation, coupled with fear and frustration.

The FLQ activists were denounced as assassins unworthy of citizenship. The future jurors who would ultimately pass judgment on the members of the Chénier Cell were convinced that they were dealing with a new species of barbarians. Their view and that of the majority was shaped by the official version of the case. Due to the sudden collapse of all opposition, this version was disseminated to the exclusion of all others.

*Louis Martin, ''Le vrai complot'', *Le Magazine Maclean,* November 1975.

Now considered an absolute evil, the FLQ became a convenient target. Its clandestine nature and scant resources placed it completely at the mercy of the political cynicism of the powers that be.

As we have seen previously, the FLQ had never really taken the initiative in the crisis. It had fallen head-first into a carefully built trap.

Under the rule of the War Measures and after Laporte's death, how could the 1970 kidnappers (about ten people) have found the means and the accomplices to fight back against the devastating propaganda machine developed by those in power to justify Operation Essay? And even if they could have, who would have listened to them or believed them?

Still, the FLQ had nothing to gain if one of the hostages were killed or died accidentally. As Laporte's old friends now say, the FLQ members could not be "as crazy" as the authorities led people to believe.

For the FLQ, killing Laporte amounted to political suicide. In addition, it left all progressive forces in Quebec completely exposed to massive repression. The imposition of the War Measures the previous day removed any doubt about that.

Neither the FLQ nor the people of Quebec had anything to gain from Laporte's assassination. The federal government, on the other hand, stood to benefit immensely from a murder occurring at such a psychologically favorable time.

Mr. Ryan and his Friends

Politically, the FLQ had no reason to want Laporte to die, since a broad coalition had emerged in Quebec, pressing for serious negotiations on the release of the political prisoners.

The three labour federations, the Parti Québécois, prominent figures in the church and the universities, the newspaper *Le*

Devoir and others had joined forces to exert mounting pressure — and publicly — on the authorities. Those who were called "Mr. Ryan and his friends" in Gérard Pelletier's book rejected the excuses cited by Ottawa in its flat refusal to release the political prisoners in exchange for the lives of James Cross and Pierre Laporte. Even the War Measures proclamation had not succeeded in putting an end to this coalition's pressures.

Can we believe that, by deciding to murder Laporte, the FLQ would have given the central government a tailor-made opportunity to silence this opposition, which was gaining ground even outside Quebec?

To buy time, the authorities had pretended for a few days to be willing to negotiate. The broadcasting of the FLQ manifesto had resulted in a political victory for the FLQ and for the Quebec independence movement. For Trudeau, this propaganda concession rankled. Any concession to meet the FLQ's central demand — the release of the political prisoners — would have meant a humilitating defeat for him. It would also have seriously threatened the objective of Operation Essay, an objective that Trudeau obviously could not disclose to his opponents.

And the longer things dragged on, the greater was the risk that the coalition that had taken shape in Quebec to resist the federal aggression would manage to turn the tables in favor of separatism.

The day after the imposition of the War Measures, Claude Ryan wrote in *Le Devoir* that, by resorting to such excessive measures, the federal government ran the risk of itself contributing to the rise of the independence cause. In agreement with the informal coalition, he reaffirmed that "the question of Quebec's future" should be settled in Quebec without anyone trying to impose a solution from the outside. Meanwhile, René Lévesque called on all Québécois to unite immediately, regardless of their differences or disagreements, in order to prevent Ottawa from undermining "all our chances for a future." In the House of Commons, as we have seen, the Conservatives and New Democrats were fighting the government decision.

In these circumstances, a new shock was needed to silence the opposition and rally public support for the War Measures. On the night of October 17, the news of Laporte's assassination provided that shock. The Trudeau government's "political genius" triumphed as never before.

"Mr Ryan and his friends" might as well go into hiding to ruminate on their "shame". In the eyes of the federal authorities, they had become accomplices of banditry and assassination. At the very least, they were considered guilty of "criminal indulgence".

Ottawa remained immune to what it regarded as their weak-kneed wailings. But Parti Québécois leader René Lévesque described the federal efforts to restore democratic order in Canada as "Trudeau's filthy tactics" (*La Presse,* November 9, 1970).

"We know today that Lévesque's 'clandestine friends' were common murderers," wrote Secretary of State Gérard Pelletier in his retrospective on the events of October 1970.* "Of course," the former minister adds in his book, "the party (the PQ) can take shelter behind dialectical argument and claim that it cannot be held *responsible* for the crimes that some madman might commit in the name of the independence of Quebec. . . . But the strategy of the PQ since its creation has been to convince the population it was the only political movement openly and unequivocally advocating the independence of Quebec." Pelletier argues that the confusion in public opinion between the PQ and "a terrorist movement that claims to be fighting for independence" was the inevitable result of the PQ's "own propaganda . . . this confusion is basic to the situation."† Machiavellian

---

* Pelletier, *The October Crisis,* p. 181.
† *Ibid.,* p. 183.

thinking evidently can be carried a long way.

Laporte's death prompted Trudeau to comment on October 18 that it must not be regarded as a "pointless tragedy" but as "*a landmark* in the crusade for Canadian unity."

The exploitation of Pierre Laporte's death was certainly a towering landmark in the federal aggression against Quebec.

Now that one of the hostages had been "murdered by the FLQ," and therefore by separatism, the cabinet seemed fully justified in refusing to negotiate with "criminals" and opposition turned into support for Trudeau. Operation Essay could continue in the guise of a manhunt. Laporte's alleged kidnappers could only hide, whether they were guilty or not, since they were targets for the rage and vengeance of all the democrats in the country.

Members of the Chénier Cell, convicted by the authorities and the public without benefit of a trial, were condemned to run for cover. Needless to say, they were in no position to speak out against the "official version" of the events that had occurred in quick succession since October 5. The "organized escalation", as Laporte put it in one of his notes, had gone so far that it would not have been very surprising if another Jack Ruby had taken the law into his own hands.

Officially, Laporte's alleged kidnappers and killers were being sought all the way to Mexico, even though they could have been arrested without any trouble in the hours that followed the kidnapping, as we shall see below.

And these arrests would not have involved any loss of face for the Trudeau cabinet, just as there was no loss of face later when James Cross was released and members of the Liberation Cell were sent into exile. But could the proclamation of the War Measures Act have been justified after such arrests?

Further, if by chance some misguided policemen had picked up Paul Rose and his group on October 11, how could the authorities have explained the continued sequestration of Laporte? How could they have claimed, as Bourassa did on October 11, that the "preservation of public order" rested on him?

There is no evidence which demonstrates conclusively any official involvement in Laporte's "execution"; on the other hand, when a government prepares for the invocation of the War Measures Act five months ahead of time, we must consider how far it is prepared to go. And also, as we shall see later, no evidence was ever produced at the FLQ trials that Paul Rose and his associates took part in Laporte's murder. Nonetheless, three of them were sentenced to life imprisonment or twenty years on the strength of "trial by the press." As for Jacques Rose, who went on trial after the others and was represented by counsel, he was cleared by juries of the murder, kidnapping and sequestration charges pending against him; and these acquittals were based on the same circumstantial evidence that had been introduced at the trials of Paul Rose, Francis Simard and Bernard Lortie. The only conviction against Jacques Rose came on a belated charge of having helped his brother to escape arrest. Significantly, the Crown decided against filing appeals after Jacques Rose's three acquittals.

These later acquittals didn't matter to the federal authorities, since their most powerful scenario had become reality on October 17, 1970. At the Strategic Operations Center, the experts had rated every possible development in the crisis according to a "plus or minus" political scoring system. Thus, if Laporte or Cross were to die, this was a "plus" for Ottawa. If the murder victim's body was mutilated, this was worth two "plus" points for Ottawa, and so on.*

But if Pierre Laporte had survived his ordeal and returned to

* Louis Martin, *op. cit.*

the Quebec National Assembly, Ottawa might have lost several points and perhaps the "game".

The Official Version of the "Optimum" Scenario

For the success of the federal plan, as it was being played out by the SOC, it was important to remove from the hands of "uncontrollable" persons the power to decide whether Laporte should be released or not. The labour minister appeared to have grasped this quickly when he suggested within twenty-four hours of his kidnapping that his fate rested, not in the hands of the FLQ, but rather in those of the Quebec government. He argued in his letter that Quebec could still put an end to the "well-organized escalation" and thus avoid "a quite useless panic," on condition that police stop acting "without your (Bourassa's) knowledge." It was clear to Laporte that the continuation of police operations amounted to his "death warrant". Nowhere in this letter did he even refer to the FLQ or compare his fate to that of James Cross.

As we have seen, the "well-organized escalation" of October 1970 had been deliberately brought about by the federal government. For the provincial authorities, as Claude Ryan commented in *Le Devoir* on October 17, 1970, this situation was "a unique opportunity to assert the prerogatives of the Quebec government at the highest level." In other words, the time had come for the elected leaders of Quebec to take the lead in a mass resistance to the federal aggression.

But Bourassa had already sold out to the federal authorities. Like them, and unlike Laporte, the premier could believe that the "sacrifice" of his cabinet colleague on the altar of the supremacy of the State was essential to preserve public order.

The late minister's friends contend that "preservation of public order" through the imposition of the War Measures condemned Laporte to a "tragic fate", which the authorities stage-managed "day by day, hour by hour," between October 10 and 17, 1970.

As Roger Lemelin (publisher of *La Presse*) commented six years later, when news of Laporte's "execution" reached Ottawa late at night, the government reacted "almost with a cry of triumph" that silenced the Opposition.* The SOC scenario with the biggest political payoff had just taken place.

Laporte's body was found on federal territory on the grounds of the St. Hubert airport where a military base and Mobile Command headquarters are also located. It had been abandoned in the trunk of the very same car in which he had been abducted seven days earlier. According to a communiqué signed by an unknown cell calling itself "Dieppe (Royal 22nd)," the minister had been executed in cold blood at exactly the same time he had been abducted the previous Saturday, that is at 6:18 p.m. Some policemen told reporters that Laporte had been horribly tortured. One radio reporter even stated on the air that the minister had been allowed to "bleed to death."

The public was horrified.

Monday's newspapers commented on how daring Laporte's kidnappers had been — they had abandoned his body under the noses of troops in battle dress at St. Hubert, as if the War Measures Act had never been invoked. On top of that, they had used the same car that had been used in the kidnapping; the licence number (9J-2420) and description of the car had been widely publicized for seven days.

A few hundred yards from the Mobile Command military headquarters, on federal territory at the height of the general mobilization, in broad daylight on October 17, the kidnappers, whoever they were, managed to drive in and out completely unnoticed. And, as we now know, as early as October 11, police knew the identities of Laporte's alleged kidnappers and were

La Presse, October 2, 1976.

tailing them as they travelled around the South Shore and Montreal (see p. 104). Paul and Jacques Rose even visited their mother on Wednesday, October 14, without showing any signs of nervousness, as Mrs. Rose testified at the coroner's inquest.

All in all, it is clear that the alleged kidnappers were unbelievably lucky. This is especially so since, well before the October crisis, the military intelligence service had reported that the FLQ activists were remarkable for their "high degree of amateurism." Contradicting the armed forces' evaluation, Jean Marchand proclaimed on October 16 in the Commons that the FLQ had even infiltrated the police.

On October 19 at 11:00 a.m., the parliamentary debate on the imposition of the War Measures Act resumed. At noon, the action was approved by a vote of 190 to 16. T. C. Douglas called on potential informers to come forward in exchange for a reward. Solicitor-General McIlraith later replied that the government had "good reasons not to offer a reward." But early in November, Ottawa and Quebec offered a joint reward of $150,000 for information on the Cross kidnapping.

In the hours that followed Laporte's death, the police issued warrants for the arrests of Paul Rose and Marc Carbonneau. Strangely, however, no such warrants were issued for Jacques Lanctôt, who had been linked to the kidnap plots back on October 5, or for Jacques Rose, Francis Simard, Bernard Lortie and the others, even though police forces had their descriptions, pictures and detailed files on their activities, habits and hangouts.

For Operation Essay to succeed, mystery had to be maintained as long as possible. Long enough, at least, to convince the public that the FLQ represented a formidable organization in 1970, while leading people to believe that law-enforcement agencies were ill-prepared to cope with a situation unprecedented in Canadian history.

At regular intervals, however, the Quebec Police director announced publicly that the investigation was progressing. And, in fact, the official scenario was gradually taking shape, fueled by calculated "disclosures".

One such "disclosure" came after police issued pictures of Paul Rose and Marc Carbonneau, who were officially "wanted in connection with the kidnappings of James Cross and Pierre Laporte." On October 19, police "discovered" the house at 5630 Armstrong Street, near the St. Hubert base, as a result of "an anonymous phone call" and they announced that Laporte had been held hostage and murdered there.

After dynamiting the doors of the house open and *before* police technicians could check the house for fingerprints and other evidence, detectives flatly told a horde of newsmen attracted by the military show that Laporte had been taken to the bungalow immediately after being kidnapped, that he had been held there for a week and had died there. But they added that no traces of blood had been found and that it would be practically impossible to gather valid evidence in the house, due to the "explosive" nature of the raid.

The numerous pictures taken that day by police photographers show that the raiding party left the interior of the house in a complete shambles.

Could such unorthodox investigative methods be aimed at establishing the truth or collecting pertinent clues?

Nevertheless, the "discovery" of the house in St. Hubert received massive publicity. Police spread rumours that Laporte had been morbidly tortured and allowed to bleed to death — all this in a house where members of the raiding party said there appeared to be no signs of blood. At the FLQ trials much later, police witnesses said they had found spots of blood.

On October 21, there was another disclosure: the minister had been neither tortured nor mutilated, but strangled with his own neck chain. Pathologists placed the time of death *somewhere* between 12:00 noon and 11:00 p.m. on October 17.

The pathologists also reported that Laporte had lost blood from three different wounds "before his death," but that this was not the cause of death. The "preliminary" autopsy report dismissed these wounds as "rather superficial cuts and scratches." On November 7, Bernard Lortie was called as a witness at the inquest, where he testified that Laporte had cut himself by trying to leap through a window the day before he died. Later, Lortie said he had been "forced to invent a story" at the inquest.

Laporte did not appear to have lost weight during his captivity since his body weighed 178 pounds at the autopsy. At the time he was kidnapped he weighed 180 pounds, according to the description issued by Quebec Police on October 10.

From then on, the authorities claimed that they had revealed the causes and circumstances of the kidnapping, sequestration and murder of Laporte. Their version was not founded on any hard evidence, but that did not seem to matter. In late December, police arrested the Rose brothers and Francis Simard. Since their "guilt" could not be established except through "confessions", due to the lack of hard evidence, detectives took it upon themselves to draft statements for the accused. These unsigned "confessions" enabled the special coroner to wind up his inquest and to find the members of the Chénier Cell "criminally responsible" for Laporte's death. To avoid any possibility of embarrassments, Paul Rose, the alleged leader of the Chénier Cell, was excluded from the courtroom during most of his trial. It seems he grew angry too often.

The armed forces returned to their bases early in 1971 and the Laporte case was soon considered closed. Many questions remained unanswered, but every time they have been raised over the years, the authorities have replied that the case is closed and that the courts have condemned the guilty.

As for the bitter criticism voiced by the friends of the Laporte family since 1970, it has been brushed aside by those in power as the product of "paranoid phobias".

But the questions persist. In recent years, many journalists have reached the conclusion that these questions are too serious to remain unanswered and that the official version disseminated in 1970 does not stand up. That is why it becomes important to scrutinize one by one the facts relating to the kidnapping, sequestration and death of Pierre Laporte. This is the object of the following pages.

When Kidnappers Have Incredible Luck

The most amazing thing about the Laporte kidnapping is the ease with which it was pulled off. On October 10, Laporte was not only the government House leader but the acting premier of Quebec in the absence of Robert Bourassa. Five days after the James Cross kidnapping and despite rumours about an "escalation" that could lead to "political assassinations", the Laporte residence was left without any police protection.

On October 6, the day after the abduction of the British diplomat, some newspapers reported that many important Quebec politicians were on "the list of FLQ targets." *La Presse* specified that a document that had been seized by the police lent weight to the theory that the Cross kidnapping would be followed by "selective assassinations". The newspaper speculated that an escalation could go far as slayings of leading politicians. The Montreal *Gazette* also referred to the danger of an escalation, adding that many politicians were already receiving special protection. (The day before, the federal government had given assurances that representatives of foreign countries were getting "extra protection".)

On October 7, *Le Devoir* quoted Premier Bourassa as saying

that "special measures for the protection of public figures are certainly not superfluous." The same day, in Quebec, *Le Soleil* reported that Bourassa had made it clear that protection of Quebec politicians would be strengthened. "It is only normal to protect public figures right now," the premier was quoted as saying, "since we are experiencing a rather difficult period in that regard."

Also on October 7, a police spokesman stated that many officers from the RCMP, Quebec Police and Montreal Police had been assigned to new duties as bodyguards or lookouts around certain homes and buildings. Finally, *Le Journal de Montréal* reported that security had been tightened the previous day in the Quebec National Assembly building and that all persons entering committee rooms had to show identity cards.

On October 8, *Le Soleil* noted in a dispatch from Ottawa that on the previous day, "Prime Minister Trudeau's limousine was escorted for the first time by two unmarked police cars." As for Bourassa, he went to New York for several days of talks with investors, and Laporte took over in Quebec as acting premier. How was it that the ranking government figure did not receive special protection after three full days of crisis?

Along with Bourassa and Choquette, the labour minister certainly was a likely target for a kidnap or murder attempt. He was considered the "strongman" of the cabinet, much more experienced in government and politics than the premier.

According to RCMP sources, no fewer than twenty-two cells of the FLQ were ready to swing into action, as the *Gazette* reported on October 16. Furthermore, since the summer of 1970, the police and the armed forces had warned political leaders about the possibility of assassination attempts in the fall.*

What explanation is there for the fact that on October 10, when Laporte was abducted, not a single policeman was in the vicinity

*CBC, *Background to Military Role* (unpublished), p. 11.

of the minister's home? It is especially baffling, since he was at that time the subject of scrutiny and protection from three different police forces.

Caught completely by surprise, Chief Gerald Reilly of the St. Lambert police department said after the kidnapping that his men had kept a special watch on the Laporte residence. He added, however, that this did not mean that surveillance was maintained "twenty-four hours a day."

Soon after the abduction, a St. Lambert policeman stated that the neighbourhood where the minister lived was "patrolled constantly by the police."* Local police did in fact carry out special patrols near Laporte's home at regular intervals every day; patrols were increased when the minister was home.

Chief Inspector Paul Benoit of the Quebec Police disclosed later that Laporte had been the target of several threats before being kidnapped.†

On October 12, the Montreal newspapers, particularly the *Star* and the *Gazette*, reported that many of the Laportes' neighbours recalled having seen parked cars near the minister's home in the days preceding his abduction (and also in the days that preceded the return of the Rose brothers and Francis Simard from Texas). According to the *Star*, a dark Chevrolet had been noticed every day since Wednesday, October 7. Other neighbours said they had seen strangers with motorcycles loitering in the area.

On October 10, Laporte came home at about 5:30 p.m. About forty-five minutes later, he walked out the front door and waited outside for his wife to join him, as they were to dine out with friends. Once outside, he walked to the sidewalk to catch a football that his nephew tossed at him. He hardly had time to set foot on the sidewalk before the kidnappers' car pulled up.

*The Montreal Star, October 12, 1970.
† Ibid.

Answering a call, police got confused about the address, as in the Cross kidnapping, and went to the wrong house.

At the time of the Laporte kidnapping, had all the policemen patrolling the streets of St. Lambert been allowed to have dinner together? What kind of "special surveillance" were they providing for the minister? Which police force was in charge of this surveillance? Why did this surveillance suddenly stop on October 10 just when unknown individuals decided to abduct the most important member of the cabinet next to the premier?

The previous month, the Quebec Police had decided on its own initiative to give Laporte special protection after receiving information that was deemed serious enough to warrant security measures. One of the minister's friends had received calls from two men seeking information about Laporte's home. Finding these calls suspicious, he had informed one of the minister's aides, who in turn had advised a senior officer in the QPF. The decision to provide protection for Laporte had been made instantly.*

Police can protect a minister discreetly, without necessarily assigning a bodyguard, but this kind of minimum measure would not be termed "special protection". The decision to protect Laporte was reached in September. Wasn't this step all the more necessary five days after the Cross kidnapping?

Meanwhile, despite the kidnap crisis, the Operation Vegas investigation into organized crime was continuing, at least during the first week. Since the summer of 1969, undercover policemen working on this vast wiretapping and surveillance operation had shown special interest in Laporte and some of his

---

* This has been corroborated by several reliable sources. About the same time, an underground newspaper *La Claque* (a colloquialism which means striking a blow) appeared on the streets with the green, white and red stripes of the *Patriote* flag of 1837. A lengthy front page article spoke vaguely about a "fall offensive" and ended with the cryptic expression *à la porte,* which could have been a pun on the minister's name.

political organizers, including Jean-Jacques Côté and René Gagnon.* Many police reports had been filed about them, particularly relating to the Quebec Liberal leadership race and the financing of Laporte's campaign. One of these reports, dated September 17, 1970, and signed by Corporal R.G. Lagimodière and Constable J.O.C. Vachon stated, among other things, that Laporte's organization had received cash contributions from Montreal organized crime figures. This report was quoted by Nick Auf der Maur in the September 1973 issue of *Last Post* magazine. Auf der Maur's lengthy article incorporated material from numerous accounts in *Le Devoir, La Presse* and the *Toronto Star* and his own sources. He reported that Laporte's links with various leading racketeers in 1969 and 1970 had been described by the Operation Vegas investigators in at least eighteen separate reports.

In an interview with a CBC researcher in May 1975, former Ontario Attorney-General Arthur Wishart disclosed that during the October Crisis he had been briefed on the Laporte affair by the Ontario Provincial Police. He gained the impression that Laporte was a Liberal party bagman with mysterious connections who might have got into trouble because of large amounts of money he collected during the 1970 election campaign from shady sources.

Two senior officials of the Quebec government gave similar accounts in separate interviews with the author in November 1975. They said that money raised by Laporte failed to reach Liberal party coffers, and suggested that this sparked a power struggle within the Party, culminating in a "political contract" for a gangland execution of the minister disguised as an FLQ assassination. As for Wishart, he instructed the Ontario Provin-

* Jean-Pierre Charbonneau, *The Canadian Connection*, Optimum Books Ltd., Montreal, 1976, p. 492. (Originally *La filière canadienne*, Editions de l'homme, 1975.)

cial Police in 1970 to have nothing to do with the operations launched under the terms of the War Measures Act. The CBC researchers obtained a copy of Wishart's directives to the OPP.

If the interpretations made by the former attorney-general of Ontario and by the two senior Quebec officials are accurate, could it be that a connection existed between the information gathered by the Operation Vegas team and Laporte's kidnapping?

When Bourassa was appointing his cabinet after winning the April 1970 election, he was informed, along with his top aide, Paul Desrochers, and Jérôme Choquette, of Laporte's links with organized crime bosses. They knew perfectly well that the reports drafted by the Operation Vegas investigators amounted to political dynamite. Laporte himself may have learned that the police were investigating his activities when he failed to get the cabinet portfolio he wanted — justice.

Shortly before the October crisis, the Operation Vegas team (including men from the Quebec Police under the command of Inspector Hervé Patenaude) was building a case that threatened to lead eventually to criminal charges against Laporte. The top figures in the Liberal Party naturally feared such a development.*

Several journalists began uncovering indications that a scandal was brewing. Needless to say, relations between Choquette and Laporte became very tense. We will return to this aspect of the Laporte case later.

Suffice it to say at this point that on October 5 and 6, 1970, members of the Operation Vegas team were in the vicinity of Laporte's home to observe certain establishments on Taschereau

---

* Nick Auf def Maur, "L'affaire Laporte", *Last Post*, Volume 3, Number 5, September 1973, p. 25. Coming out of a meeting where the possibility of negotiating for Laporte's release had been discussed, Choquette told Bourassa: "It's me or him. In any case, Laporte is finished."

Boulevard, where shady individuals connected with Laporte's political organization congregated. These individuals included Frank Dasti (now serving a twenty-year prison sentence in the U.S. for heroin smuggling).* One of the officers taking part in this stake-out was Corporal Lagimodière, co-author of the September 17 report mentioned above. He was accompanied at one point by Constable Kevin Gallagher.

It should be pointed out that the Operation Vegas investigators and supervisors had no official role in the investigation into the James Cross kidnapping, although this may have changed after Laporte was abducted. At any rate, we can presume that the Vegas unit maintained a special surveillance of the Laporte circle until October 10.

By an odd coincidence, a Sergeant Desjardins who took charge of the St. Lambert police investigation into the minister's abduction (as reported by the *Montreal Star* on October 12) was described in an RCMP report dated April 22, 1971, as an investigator "attached to the Quebec Research Bureau on Organized Crime." This was precisely the police unit that was primarily responsible for Operation Vegas (see note on p. 100). The same Sergeant Desjardins told the *Montreal Star* on the night of the Laporte kidnapping that the minister's neighborhood had been patrolled regularly.†

In short, as a result of rather special circumstances, Laporte was being watched by the Operation Vegas unit in October 1970; moreover, the Quebec Police had deemed it necessary the previous month to give him special protection because of certain information it had received; the Cross kidnapping and Laporte's important duties in the Quebec government made this protection even more necessary; finally, the minister's neighborhood was being patrolled regularly by the police.

* Jean-Pierre Charbonneau, *op. cit.,* p. 339.
† *The Montreal Star,* October 12, 1970.

How could the kidnappers get close to him so easily and disappear so quickly?

According to the official version, this lucky coup was pulled off by the Rose brothers, Francis Simard and Bernard Lortie, who made up the so-called Chénier fund-raising cell of the FLQ. They are supposed to have listened until 5:55 p.m. to a televised statement in which Justice Minister Choquette rejected the demands of the Liberation Cell, then rushed to St. Lambert to kidnap Laporte a few minutes later, just before he was to leave to dine out. Then they would have taken the minister to the house on Armstrong Street in St. Hubert without attracting any attention.

But it so happens that the Rose brothers and Simard had been kept under police surveillance since 1968 at least. Since early 1970, police also knew that they were discussing plans for a kidnapping. The aborted attempt to kidnap the U.S. consul in June 1970 had led police to their main base of operations, a farm at Ste-Anne-de-la-Rochelle in the Eastern Townships. The house on Armstrong Street was also known to the police (see page 113). In September 1970, things were going so badly for the Rose brothers and Simard that they left on a motor trip to Texas because they opposed the Liberation Cell's kidnap plans and wanted to avoid being implicated by police for something they had not done. (In an interview published in the January 1977 issue of *La Revue Châtelaine,* Mrs. Rosa Rose says that she and her sons were in fact heading for Mexico.)

However, after hearing the news about the Cross kidnapping, the Rose group turned around and returned to Longueuil as fast as it could. Again according to the official version, as soon as the Rose brothers returned home, they decided that a second kidnapping was needed to force the authorities to yield. And by a rare stroke of luck, Laporte was standing on the sidewalk ready to be picked up.

The list of ''FLQ suspects'' that police had, both before and

after the Cross kidnapping, contained *only about ten names.* *
Since October 5, police knew that the British trade commissioner
had been kidnapped by Jacques Lanctôt's group, which, as if to
remove any doubt about their involvement, had used a taxicab.
(Lanctôt and Marc Carbonneau had been publicly identified for
more than a year as the leaders of the Taxi Liberation Movement.) The only people who were "available" for a second
kidnapping were Paul Rose and his group.

Between October 5 and 10, police arrested several of the
group's friends on the South Shore and learned from them that
the Roses had travelled to the U.S. and, later, that they had
returned. It became easy for police to arrest them or follow them.

Already, a bench warrant had been issued on September 21 for
Paul Rose's arrest, because he had failed to appear in court on a
charge dating back to the St. Jean Baptiste riot in June 1968. The
next day, police had located Rose, who had appeared in court
without a lawyer. His case had been remanded again, this time
until January 7, 1971.

Shortly before October 10, police raided an apartment at 1148
Roland Therrien Boulevard in Longueuil and arrested several of
the organizers of La Maison du Pêcheur and friends of the Rose
brothers, including Normand Turgeon and Jean-Luc Arène.
Bernard Lortie also lived in that apartment.† The fact that police
had asked questions relating to Paul Rose's whereabouts during
this raid had been reported to the *Quartier Latin* newsroom at
the University of Montreal community center. After the Cross
kidnapping, the editors of *Quartier Latin* remained in close
contact with the group at the Therrien Boulevard apartment and
informed the news media about persons who were being picked

* Unpublished research materials for the 1975 CBC documentary *The October
  Crisis.*
† *La Presse,* November 9, 1970. The testimony was given at the inquest on
  November 7.

up to prevent police from holding them incommunicado. Similar liaison existed with the underground paper *La Claque*.

Since Bernard Lortie lived at the Longueuil apartment that was raided, it seems likely that he would have learned that police were quite curious, *before October 10,* about the Rose brothers and Simard. This trio returned to Longueuil on October 8 according to some witnesses, on October 9 according to a close friend of Lortie, or on October 6 according to the testimony of Pierre Lemay at the Laporte inquest.*

Whatever date was correct, certain informants say that the police knew the whereabouts of the Rose trio before the Laporte kidnapping.

If by any chance this trio, hampered as it was by its lack of means, decided to act, was there not a strong likelihood that it would try its luck on the South Shore, in or near Longueuil? Isn't it fair to assume that the specialists in the anti-subversive squad realized this? Provided, of course, that every effort was made to prevent a second kidnapping.

The armed forces intelligence service must have made the same deduction, since it had concluded that the FLQ members operated with a "high degree of amateurism."**

And we know now that the Civil Emergencies Section of the military Mobile Command exchanged all information relating to subversion — both real and potential — with the police forces on a daily basis.†

If there was a real possibility that the FLQ would strike a second time, and probably on the South Shore, the logical target was Laporte, who dominated South Shore politics as the member for Chambly. He was the only person who carried enough weight politically and whose kidnapping might force the authorities to

* Inquest proceedings, November 4, 1970.
** CBC, *Background to Military Role*, p. 11.
† *Ibid.*, p. 8.

yield. Police had obvious reasons to want to take security measures to protect him.

Did the police receive directives to allow the FLQ members to operate freely? Were they instructed on October 10 to suspend their special operations on the South Shore? Did the powers that be feel that this was a good opportunity to avoid an imminent scandal and to get rid of Laporte? Were the minister's close associates right when they later described his slaying as the result of internecine warfare in the Liberal machine? Was Laporte really kidnapped by the men whose "confessions" were introduced at the coroner's inquest by the Quebec Police? If so, did they act alone?

"Clean-cut Men with a Walkie-talkie"

Was Laporte expected by the kidnappers? There is a possibility that they were tipped off that he was about to leave his house.

According to the eyewitnesses (whose accounts contradict the "confessions" scripted by the police), the kidnappers first parked on Berkley Street, not far from the Laporte residence. At that point, "the occupants of the car were not wearing masks."* A bit later, they moved closer to the minister's home, parking on a spot on Robitaille Street from which they could see the front door. As soon as Laporte joined his nephew on the sidewalk, the car pulled up in front of him. Two masked gunmen got out, Laporte got into the car without putting up any resistance and the vehicle took off at high speed.

The witnesses only had time to note that the car was a 1968 Chevrolet bearing license plate number 9J-2420.

Sergeant Desjardins told reporters that the kidnappers' car had been seen by witnesses "before it reached Robitaille Street and until it suddenly disappeared around the corner of Logan Street

_____
* *The Montreal Star* and *The Gazette,* October 12, 1970.

and Taschereau Boulevard" in St. Lambert. All witnesses had given the same description of the car and its occupants.

The six eyewitnesses of the abduction itself (Laporte's wife and nephew and four neighbours) all stated that the kidnappers were "clean-cut" and well dressed,* which Sergeant Desjardins confirmed in an interview the same night.

Another witness, an attendant at a Taschereau Boulevard gas station, reported that shortly before the kidnapping, strangers stopped to ask him the way to Robitaille Street (where Laporte lived). "I thought they were policemen or reporters," he commented, "because one of them was carrying something that looked like a walkie-talkie."†

Two minutes after the abduction, a general alert was broadcast on police radios throughout the South Shore region and roadblocks were set up immediately on all main thoroughfares. "How the devil could the kidnappers disappear so quickly?" wondered a police official interviewed that night by Eddie Collister of *The Gazette*. Unmarked police cars maintained surveillance at all major intersections and at all bridges across the St. Lawrence. The description and license number of the 1968 Chevrolet had been flashed at the same time as the general alert. Around the St. Hubert airport, military policemen patrolled La Savanne Road and side streets where the military base personnel live.

On October 5, police had offered somewhat plausible explanations for their failure to chase the Cross kidnappers, but this time a similar failure raised more doubts.

Some policemen speculated that the Laporte kidnappers might have concealed their "hot" car in a garage near Taschereau Boulevard and switched to a safe car to take the minister to a hideout.

*Ibid.
†*The Gazette* and *La Presse,* October 12, 1970.

When the gas station attendant talked about men with a walkie-talkie, people immediately assumed that the kidnapping had been carefully planned. But in the weeks that followed, a different version emerged — the kidnapping had been improvised at the last minute and had succeeded due to extraordinary luck and daring.

A Chevrolet Marked "Rose"

According to the "full admissions" that police attributed later to Paul Rose and Francis Simard, members of the Chénier Cell are supposed to have watched Laporte's comings and goings in St. Lambert the day before the kidnapping. Actually, Laporte was in Quebec that day. As acting premier and House leader, he was completing arrangements for a special session scheduled to open the following Monday to deal with a withdrawal of services by Quebec's medical specialists. He was working with Social Affairs Minister Claude Castonguay on a draft bill compelling the doctors to end their strike.

On Saturday, October 10, Laporte met a delegation of French businessmen to urge them to invest in Quebec and thus help develop relations between France and Quebec into something more than friendly sentiments.

As mentioned previously, he arrived home around 5:30 p.m., about forty-five minutes before being abducted.

The unsigned statements attributed to members of the Chénier Cell refer to another trip that the kidnappers supposedly made to Laporte's neighborhood on the afternoon of October 10, to see if he was home. Then, after watching Choquette's appearance on television, they allegedly left the house on Armstrong Street in St. Hubert around 6:00 p.m. Once they reached Robitaille Street, the statements add, "we got the impression that there was some activity in Pierre Laporte's residence." What kind of activity?

"Then, we decided to go to Longueuil to call the house to make sure he was there."* Mrs. Laporte answered the phone and said that "her husband had just stepped outside."† After making their call from Longueuil, the four kidnappers supposedly returned to St. Lambert and abducted the minister "who was playing catch with his nephew."

How could they do all those things in such a short period of time? Why did they call at the very last minute and risk arousing suspicion?

As we have seen, Laporte was abducted as soon as he stepped on the sidewalk. He did not even have time to say one word to his nephew. We have also seen that the kidnappers' car was parked on Berkley Street before the minister came out of the house, and that they later moved to Robitaille Street while waiting for him to appear.

The 1968 Chevrolet could not be on Berkley Street in St. Lambert and near a telephone booth in Longueuil at the same time. If the kidnappers had bothered to drive back to Longueuil to make a phone call — "to make sure he was there" — and Mrs. Laporte had told them that "her husband had just stepped outside," they would have needed more time to return to the Laporte residence than it actually took to kidnap the minister. When the abduction took place, Mrs. Laporte was stepping out the door to join her husband and she saw what happened.

When accused persons make more admissions than are required for a plausible confession, the plausibility of the confession must certainly come into question.

Many reacted with skepticism, including Gaston Miron, a prominent figure in Quebec's literary and publishing circles. After making a detailed analysis of the vocabulary and style of the "confessions" attributed to Paul Rose, he came to the conclusion that at least two persons drafted the statement.

According to the "confessions" that made headlines at the time, Paul and Jacques Rose, Francis Simard and Bernard Lortie were the occupants of the 1968 Chevrolet bearing plates number 9J-2420 at the time of the kidnapping. (For some reason, in the statement attributed by the police to Paul Rose, a mysterious "Monsieur X" replaced Lortie.) The kidnappers forced Laporte at gunpoint to get into the car. They then supposedly drove along Logan Street, Tiffin Road and St. Paul Street before reaching Taschereau Boulevard. They stopped at the corner of St. Paul and Taschereau to drop off Simard so that he could plant a communiqué. (However, it would be 8:00 a.m. the following morning before a caller told a CKAC reporter that the communiqué could be found at the Peel subway station in downtown Montreal.) This communiqué would have been drafted prior to the abduction.

After stopping at the corner of St. Paul and Taschereau, an intersection near Laporte's home, and amid a general police alert, the remaining trio drove along Taschereau to the Laurier Boulevard interchange, then along Laurier to another major interchange with Chambly Road in St. Hubert. After travelling a short distance on Chambly, they turned right at La Savanne Road and crossed federal territory between the Mobile Command headquarters and the St. Hubert air base before reaching 5630 Armstrong Street.

According to the official version of the story, no police car chased them, no roadblocks were encountered at the above-mentioned interchanges, no military personnel spotted them on La Savanne Road. Still, as early as October 6, Mobile Command had ordered all military bases (including St. Hubert, of course) to set up *extra* security around their perimeters because it had reason to believe that James Cross might be taken to one of the bases eventually.* Under these orders, particular attention had to be given to *all vehicles* passing in the vicinity of the various bases.

In the hours that followed the Laporte abduction, police let it be known that the 1968 Chevrolet was registered under a false name, Paul Fournier. The owner's address was listed as 1260 Green Street, St. Lambert, three blocks from the minister's street. Police, having rushed to this address, failed to find any Paul Fournier but, according to Inspector Paul Benoit of the Quebec Police, they learned that Lise Rose had once lived there. The sister of Paul and Jacques Rose, who was a civil servant in the Quebec Revenue Department in 1970, resided at 1103 Dorion Street in Longueuil. Finally, according to evidence introduced at the Rose trials, the registration slip for the Chevrolet had been signed by Yves Langlois of the Liberation Cell, using the alias of Pierre Seguin. (Langlois, who spent more than a year in London before the 1970 crisis, is the son of a federal government official.)

According to Inspector Benoit, as soon as police checked out the Green Street address, they became convinced that Paul Rose was involved in the kidnapping and that Laporte was being held hostage somewhere on the South Shore.† The search was therefore concentrated on Longueuil and neighboring suburbs. A few days later, Paul Rose was being shadowed by unmarked police cars in Longueuil. He was not picked up for questioning or interfered with because, according to the story given later by Quebec Police officials, there was no evidence linking him with the kidnapping!

Furthermore, even though the kidnap car was registered under a fictitious name, police discovered that it had already been

___

* CBC, *Background to Military Role,* p. 11.

† Unpublished research materials for the 1975 CBC documentary *The October Crisis.*

involved in a series of traffic violations. But perhaps the license plates had been installed on a different Chevorlet. (According to the confession attributed to Paul Rose, the Chevrolet used in the kidnapping bore plates number 9K-2420, not 9J-2420. And according to friends of Rose, the group had not used that Chevrolet since the summer of 1970.)

At any rate, police connected the kidnap car with the Paul Rose group within a few hours. But they received instructions not to arrest or question Rose because there was no evidence he was involved in the kidnapping. A second explanation, given later, was that police had to avoid endangering Laporte's life. Does this in fact mean that some people in high places wanted to implicate Rose and his associates in the kidnapping, whether they were actually involved or not?

The House on Armstrong Street

If Laporte was really taken to the house at 5630 Armstrong Street, why is it that the police did not quickly surround the house and rescue him?

This question arises because there is every reason to believe that on the day Laporte was abducted, the police knew about the house in St. Hubert and that it had been rented the previous March by Paul Rose and Lise Balcer, posing as Mr. and Mrs. Paul Blais.

In this connection, an interesting Quebec Police report has come to light. The report, listing some exhibits, is dated November 5, 1970, and is annexed to file number 047-10-10-70-011 (the Laporte case, as the number based on the date of the kidnapping indicates). The following inscription appears at the top of the page: "5630 Armstrong, St. Hubert, on 10-10-70." It is difficult to tell exactly what the police did at the Armstrong Street address that day, since a few words have been crossed out. The obliteration is initialed, with the badge number 3696 appearing next to the initials. The report itself is signed by Corporal Luc Jarry of the Quebec Police (badge number 2711).

Did the police raid the house on Armstrong Street on the day Laporte was kidnapped? Did the police question the occupants of the house, who had just returned from the U.S.?

At any rate, this house was known to the police before the October crisis. Marc Carbonneau, Claude Morency and Paul Rose had been followed there, among others, along with many of those who lived at 1148 Roland Therrien Boulevard (where the residents included Bernard Lortie and Lise Balcer).

Policemen had grown more interested in the Armstrong Street house following a holdup in May 1970 attributed to the FLQ and particularly after the dismantling of the plot to kidnap the U.S. consul in June.

Inspector Robert Côté of the Montreal Police bomb squad has confirmed that this house was under police surveillance *at the time Laporte was kidnapped.* Two months before, he had received a secret report forecasting a "fall offensive by the FLQ."* Another Montreal police officer has confirmed that Claude Morency was followed by an unmarked police car to the Armstrong Street meeting place in June 1970. This occurred during the investigation that eventually led to the arrests of Morency, Francois Lanctôt and André Roy on charges of conspiring to kidnap the U.S. consul.

After the Laporte kidnapping, police went to the house in St. Hubert, but the minister was not there. About two months later, Justice Minister Choquette told a senior official of the Quebec government: "We were very unlucky in the Laporte case. While he was a hostage, police raided the house on Armstrong Street three times, but they did not find any trace of him." This fact,

Ibid.

disclosed by *Le Jour* in October 1975, has never been denied by Choquette.

Similarly, one of Mayor Jean Drapeau's top assistants recalls learning that police had conducted a raid at 5630 Armstrong Street in the days preceding Laporte's slaying. This operation had been reported by Michel Côté to certain members of the City of Montreal executive committee, in a briefing on the progress of the police investigation.* When the mayor's assistant and an executive committee member learned later that Laporte had been held hostage and murdered in that house, they were startled. "How could the police miss Laporte?" they wondered. "That house was raided!"

Unless, Unless . . .

Despite all the official accounts, could it be that Laporte was *not* held in the Armstrong Street house?

If in fact Laporte was sequestered there without interruption from October 10 to 17, how could the police have failed to rescue him? It would have been child's play for policemen and troops to storm the house. All the more so since members of the Chénier Cell, sometimes alone and sometimes together, kept travelling across the South Shore and in Montreal. This would have left very few alledged kidnappers to watch Laporte at certain points.

Thus, during the week that Laporte was held hostage, Paul and Jacques Rose visited their mother; Simard and Paul Rose went to the apartment on Queen Mary Road; and Paul Rose also visited some friends (the Venne family) and went to an office in Montreal to pay the rent for the Armstrong Street house; and Bernard Lortie left the house on October 16 to stay with friends in Montreal.† In addition, they made many trips by taxi, as several

* *Ibid.*
† Testimony at the coroner's inquest.

drivers called by the Crown testified at the FLQ trials. In some cases, particularly for Paul Rose, these movements were observed by the police.

As we have seen, it was decided in high places not to arrest Paul Rose. (This was confirmed in the Commons by Solicitor-General George McIlraith on November 2, 1970.) Yet, Rose's right thumb print was found on a communiqué dated October 11.*

In addition to the fact that police did not have conclusive proof that Paul Rose was involved in the kidnapping, since one can deliver a communiqué without being a kidnapper, it has been stated that the decision not to pick up Rose was based on the fear of endangering the lives of Laporte or Cross.

But if this is so, why did the police arrest Bernard Lortie on November 6, one month before the release of James Cross? And why did the police wait nearly two days after Laporte's slaying to announce the "discovery" of the house on Armstrong Street — where raids had been carried out the previous week?

Certain Quebec Police officers offered a less farfetched explanation in 1975: "The police did not know where Laporte was being held." But this explanation contradicts a statement made by Premier Bourassa to Mrs. Laporte on October 14, 1970. He said that the police had located the place where her husband was being held. "His release is only a question of hours," Bourassa assured her. "We are only waiting for an opportunity to intervene without endangering him."†

If, as the premier told Mrs. Laporte, the police had located the minister's place of detention on October 14, was this place really the house on Armstrong Street? If not, where was it?

---

* Exhibit PP-140 in the Quebec Appeal Court records relating to Jacques Rose, file number 10-00176-73.

† Unpublished research materials for the 1975 CBC documentary *The October Crisis*.

The raid carried out at 5630 Armstrong Street on October 19 raises many questions. First, the police created unusual disorder in the house. If there had been a possibility of finding some clues of Laporte's presence there at one point or another, would the policemen have used explosives before making their examination? Or was the disorder caused intentionally to lead people to believe later that Laporte had been involved in a brawl with his kidnappers?*

According to friends of the late minister, some policemen who took part in the October 19 raid told them that Paul Desrochers, then the top aide to Premier Bourassa, had visited the house during the raid. Why would the chief organizer of the Quebec Liberal Party have deemed such a visit necessary?

In any event, it is strange that police felt no urge, while tailing Paul Rose on the South Shore, to question him about Laporte's whereabouts. Perhaps people in high places already knew, as Bourassa said on October 14. In this case, the authorities had nothing to learn from Paul Rose and his companions. What then was the role played by the Chénier Cell in this affair? Was it a channel of communications between Laporte's "clean-cut" kidnappers and the news media? Was it caught in an ingenious trap?

Whatever role the cell played, many doubts persist about the official version of the Laporte case and the "confessions" fabricated to accommodate what Ron Haggart and Aubrey Golden term "the unjudicial process."†

Unlikely Delays

What makes the official version of the Laporte case even more unlikely is the rather bizarre chain of events surrounding the

---

* Police created similar disorder during their raid at the apartment on Queen Mary Road, as can be seen in police pictures.
† Haggart and Golden, *Rumours of War*, p. 189.

discovery of the minister's body at the St. Hubert air base on October 17, 1970.

Between 4:00 p.m. and 5:00 p.m. that day, Mrs. Laurence Sasseville, the switchboard operator and receptionist at radio station CKAC, was told by an anonymous caller that "Pierre Laporte's body" was near the Won-Del Aviation Inc. hangar at St. Hubert airport. Mrs. Sasseville immediately informed the reporters at the station and the vice-president, Philippe Germain. She relayed all the details that the caller had provided — that the body was in the trunk of a Chevrolet bearing license plates number 9J-2420 and that the keys were in the car. He had added that a communiqué giving "all the details" had been left at Place des Arts, less than a mile from the station.*

However, CKAC personnel did not take this information seriously until 9:30 p.m., more than four hours later. As for the police, they did not arrive on the scene in St. Hubert until 11:10 p.m. After waiting for military personnel, police officially found Laporte's body at five minutes past midnight, that is, *more than seven hours* after the call received by Mrs. Sasseville.

How can such long delays be explained, especially considering the fact that the body was at the St. Hubert airport, just a short distance from the Mobile Command headquarters?

CKAC spokesmen explained the station's skeptical reaction by noting that immediately after the original call, an unusually large number of anonymous calls were received, claiming that both Laporte and Cross had been killed. "We felt at that point that crackpots were trying to fool us," Mrs. Sasseville recalls.

It should be remembered, however, that Justice Minister Choquette had met executives from all the news media that morning at the Queen Elizabeth Hotel to urge them to adopt "strict discipline". Did the CKAC management await the green light

* See the series on October 1970 published by *Le Jour* in October and November 1975.

from the police before sending a reporter to St. Hubert?

We can presume that after the call reported by Mrs. Sasseville, CKAC newsmen tried to get a confirmation or additional details from the Quebec Police, as is the practice in such circumstances.

At any rate, the CKAC management definitely appears to have taken the call seriously, since it called in a reporter who had taken the day off. (The reporter confirmed this fact in November 1975.) He was told then by his superiors, "Laporte is dead." But when he reached the station, he was told that the news was unconfirmed and that it might prove to be a false alarm.

Since October 15, reports had been circulating among journalists that Laporte was being held somewhere in St. Hubert. One report had it that he was in a deserted area near a church and the St. Hubert air base. Three reporters from the CBC French network tried vainly to find such a location shortly before the proclamation of the War Measures Act.

Like many of their colleagues, CKAC reporters likely heard these stories, which circulated persistently after October 15. Why then did the station wait so long before sending a newsman to St. Hubert?

Also, why did it take the police nearly one hour to respond to a call from Michel Saint-Louis, the CKAC reporter who found the Chevrolet? And once they arrived in St. Hubert, why did the policemen waste another hour waiting for armed forces explosives specialists to come and pry open the trunk of the Chevrolet?

Another question comes to mind: when Mrs. Sasseville received the anonymous call around 4:00 p.m., was Laporte still alive? The autopsy report, which will be analyzed further on, does not enable us to answer that question. At first, the time of death was placed somewhere between *12:00 noon and 11:00 p.m.,* and later, between *3:00 p.m. and 9:00 p.m.* In theory at least, it is possible that Laporte was alive when Michel Saint-Louis of CKAC and Robert Nadon of *La Presse* located the car

at the St.Hubert airport. But the newsmen could not find any
keys to open the trunk.

Around 9:00 p.m., even before Saint-Louis and Nadon
reached the scene, Dr. Yvon Prévost, an armed forces medical
officer, was instructed to report to the Mobile Command headquarters and to stand by for "a special duty."* He was not told
anything more and, at five minutes past midnight, he was summoned to inspect Laporte's body which was "near Hangar 12 at
the St. Hubert base," as he testified at the inquest. For three
hours he had been left alone in a room wondering what was
expected of him.**

Why did the armed forces call Dr. Prévost to St.Hubert at nine
o'clock? He certainly was not told to stand by for "a special
duty" merely to identify a Chevrolet.

It was after Dr. Prévost's arrival at the Mobile Command
headquarters that CKAC executives finally decided to send
Saint-Louis to Place des Arts to pick up the communiqué signed
by the Dieppe (Royal 22nd) Cell, then to the St. Hubert airport to
look for the car in which the body had been abandoned.

While the confirmation of Laporte's "execution" was being
delayed in this way, Justice Minister Choquette was conferring
with the co-ordinator of Operation Vegas, Chief Inspector Hervé
Patenaude.† And at 11:30 p.m., Premier Bourassa issued a
lengthy statement offering safe conduct out of the country to the
Cross and Laporte kidnappers.††

---

* Unpublished research materials for the 1975 CBC documentary *The October
Crisis*.
** Dr. Yvon Prévost later accompanied the Cross kidnappers on their military
flight to Cuba.
† Unpublished research materials for the 1975 CBC documentary *The October
Crisis*.
†† For the full text of this offer see John Saywell, *op. cit.*, p. 101.

Dieppe (Royal 22nd)

When CKAC newsmen studied the communiqué found at Place des Arts, they were puzzled by the reference to a new cell called "Dieppe (Royal 22nd)". None of the calls received by the station had referred to this name, nor to the Chénier Cell for that matter. Normand Maltais, the station's senior reporter, recalls that he did not believe the message until Laporte's body was found.

At radio station CKLM, newsmen were equally puzzled. At noon, they had received a tenth communiqué from the Liberation Cell, which stated in part: "As for Pierre Laporte, the "Chénier" cell (quotation marks were used) of the FLQ is now studying his status and will make its decision known soon." However, responsibility for Laporte's "execution" was not claimed by the Chénier Cell, but by a third cell, unknown until then.

Police prohibited the publication of the Liberation Cell's tenth communiqué, which stated that James Cross was considered a "political prisoner" but that the FLQ had no intention of endangering him and still less of "executing" him.

The Liberation Cell's message also accused the federal government of staging a "coup" and urged the media to denounce Ottawa's role.

But CKLM did not broadcast a word about this communiqué, heeding a request by the police, who argued that the War Measures regulations made it an offence to "communicate" FLQ messages. The communiqué was finally made public on December 8, after Cross was released.

At the Mobile Command communications centre in St. Hubert, a soldier on duty found the news of the minister's death even more puzzling. This French-speaking serviceman posted to the centre had received *around noon* an anonymous call almost identical to the one received about four hours later by Mrs. Sasseville at CKAC. The caller said Laporte was in the trunk of a Chevrolet parked near the Won-Del Aviation hangar at St. Hubert airport, but he did not refer to any communiqué. (When Mrs. Sasseville made her disclosures in an interview with *Le Jour* in 1975, she did not know about the similar call received at the Mobile Command communications centre, which the serviceman had reported to a few close friends shortly after Laporte's death.)

After receiving the anonymous call, the startled serviceman immediately notified his superior, an English-speaking officer, who said the message would be relayed promptly "through normal channels." But the officer ordered the serviceman to refrain from telling anyone about the call and advised him to dismiss the subject from his mind.

When Laporte's body was found, the French-speaking serviceman blurted out to a friend: "My God! The army might have saved his life if it had acted. He had been there since noon!"

Indeed, why didn't the armed forces intervene earlier? And just what did the communiqué mean by stating that Laporte "has been executed . . . by the Dieppe (Royal 22nd) Cell"?

If Laporte was in fact trapped in the trunk of the Chevrolet starting around noon on October 17, there is a real possibility that he died on federal territory at St. Hubert airport, sometime "between noon and 11:00 p.m.," as the preliminary autopsy report put it.

When the Dieppe (Royal 22nd) communiqué was read on the air, people could not help recalling that the Royal 22nd Regiment had been assigned a few days earlier to take up positions throughout the Montreal region.

Certainly, Quebec Police officers took a long time to reach the location where Saint-Louis was waiting. And the armed forces, which had installations only a few hundred yards away, took

even more time. One wonders what Dr. Prévost must have
thought when he was summoned just after midnight to pronounce
Laporte dead. And what he thought six weeks later when he
accompanied the Liberation Cell members on their flight to
Cuba, aboard a military aircraft.

Saint-Louis has stated that he found the Chevrolet without any
trouble after studying the communiqué attributed to the mysterious Dieppe Cell. Did he not in fact owe his discovery to information that had been received earlier by CKAC? Unlike the call
received by Mrs. Sasseville during the afternoon, the
communiqué did not refer to Won-Del Aviation and it said
nothing about keys being left in the car (for which Saint-Louis
hunted vainly). The "map" drawn at the bottom of the
communiqué was so vague that it made it difficult to go directly
to the right spot, which was unlit at night.

The communiqué referred only to "the St. Hubert base." The
only precise fact was license number 9J-2420. The time given for
the "execution": "6:18." seems to have been invented to coincide with the time of Laporte's kidnapping the previous Saturday. In this case, the time is given according to English-language
usage, with a period instead of an "h".

Why is it that the police authorized the broadcast and publication of this communiqué, when they had prohibited the broadcast
of the Liberation Cell communiqué on CKLM around noon the
same day?

And why is it that, after learning of the existence of the Dieppe
communiqué, police did not accompany Saint-Louis to St.
Hubert?

Isn't it also strange that Saint-Louis, having reached the scene
shortly after 10:00 p.m. and having witnessed the identification
of the body around midnight, waited for official permission from
Captain Raymond Bellemare of the Quebec Police before reporting Laporte's death on the air?

At any rate, Louis-Bernard Robitaille summed up the situation in *La Presse* on October 19, observing that "CKAC played a crucial role in the final act of the Laporte tragedy."

Another strange thing about October 17 is that no other news media were notified that Laporte's body was at St. Hubert. Maltais (who arrived at the CKAC studios at 7:00 p.m.) and Saint-Louis (who arrived about two hours later) have both stressed the fact that the anonymous caller or callers were getting increasingly impatient that evening. In the first call Maltais received, he was startled to hear this bizarre question: "Do you want Laporte's body, or don't you?"

If the caller felt then that CKAC was not reacting quickly enough, why didn't he call another station or a newspaper? Was it absolutely necessary that Laporte's body be "discovered" by CKAC reporters?

Maltais has explained his skepticism by noting that the caller or callers did not speak like the FLQ members or intermediaries who had called the station in the previous days, nor did they follow the same methods.

Skepticism, incredulity . . . these were the explanations given by the CKAC people for their slowness to react on October 17. But can skepticism or incredulity also explain the incredible slowness of the police and the armed forces on that day?

If the communiqué found at Place des Arts seemed "authentic" at 9:30 p.m., would it not have looked just as authentic at 4:00 p.m.? In this case, of course, the time of the "execution" could not have been given as 6:18 p.m. Perhaps we could have learned something else, however. For example, that Laporte was still alive when he was put in the trunk of the car, or that the FLQ had nothing to do with the decision of "the powers that be to sign Pierre Laporte's death warrant."* In short, perhaps we could

* Jean-Claude Trait, *FLQ 70: offensive d'automne,* Editions de l'homme, 1971, p. 142.

have learned "all the details" promised in the call to Mrs. Sasseville at 4:00 p.m., but which CKAC neglected to follow up by sending a reporter to Place des Arts immediately.

But as Louis-Bernard Robitaille observed, the situation was no longer the same that Saturday. Discipline prevailed. And the rules of that discipline were drawn up by the powers that be.

One indication of the highly persuasive nature of the directives given that day at CKAC is that Mrs. Laurence Sasseville waited five years before revealing what she knew, and that she did so only after consulting her union's legal adviser.

Those who knew something about the real circumstances of Laporte's slaying must have come under even more intense pressure.

That was not the time to raise questions about the behavior of the police and the armed forces. The media were expected to refrain from asking too many questions. After all, a state of war had just been proclaimed and one does not ask law enforcement agencies to justify their actions in a state of war. All their actions come under the blanket authority of national security.

And so, as the authorities wished, the Dieppe (Royal 22nd) Cell was unanimously equated with the Chénier Fund-Raising Cell. Laporte's alleged assassins were designated long before they were charged. Not only designated, but convicted.

In October 1970, Canada could not be compared with the military dictatorship in Greece but, in practice, the investigation into the Laporte "execution" was very reminiscent of the one into the 1963 assassination of the parliamentarian Lambrakis, which inspired the book and the film entitled *Z*.

On October 27, an FLQ communiqué was received which could have prompted public opinion to question the role played by those responsible for the October crisis, but police banned its publication, dismissing it as "the same old stuff." This communiqué, attributed to Paul Rose, made a connection between Dieppe and being *"forced* to serve as guinea pigs." The words "were forced" were underlined in the message. Did this mean that Operation Essay forced the Québécois to serve as guinea pigs in a military "exercise", or that the FLQ members had been forced in October to become guinea pigs in a federal machination? Or did it mean that all Québécois had been bamboozled by a massive political-military operation, a form of "official terrorism" designed to undermine their future prospects and force them to reject forever "any thought of liberation"? In any event, the FLQ did not claim the responsibility for Laporte's death.*

We have already noted that the FLQ could not expect to gain anything from the death of either hostage in 1970. On the other hand, the federal government stood to gain, since a murder helped to justify the state of war and to discredit the independence movement as a criminal conspiracy and a threat to democracy.

The suppressed communiqué of October 27 indicates that the FLQ realized perfectly well that a trap had been set for the Québécois.

Besides, didn't the October 17 communiqué already indicate, by attributing the Laporte "execution" to a third party (the Dieppe Royal 22nd Cell), that the Chénier Cell did not play any role in the murder, even if it really took part in the minister's kidnapping?

Certainly, one wonders how Paul Rose and his companions could have kept Laporte confined for one week in a house known to the police. And how they could have taken his body to St. Hubert airport in the "hottest" car in the country, right under the armed forces' noses. And of course, as was revealed at the inquest, Paul Rose knew he was being shadowed by the police.

In such circumstances, unfavourable to say the least, if the

* The full text of this communiqué appears in Trait, *op. cit.*, p. 179.

Rose group still had decided to kill Laporte to defy the "arrogance" of the federal government, wouldn't it have claimed responsibility for this act of defiance? In fact, the group did nothing of the kind. On the contrary, its members have always denied strenuously the "confessions" that police attributed to them against their will in the weeks that followed.

Later, some policemen and some Liberal politicians claimed that Laporte's death had resulted from an accident. Warren Allmand, then Solicitor-General of Canada, adopted this version in the Commons on July 23, 1973, during debate on the abolition of capital punishment. But he did not explain why the federal authorities had maintained in 1970 that Laporte had been murdered in cold blood by "separatists". Nor did he conclude that Judge Trahan's inquest and the 1971 trials of Paul Rose, Francis Simard and Bernard Lortie should be reopened, which would have been the logical result of his statement.

Allmand's remarks comprised two elements: first, Laporte's death had not been premeditated; second, he had died by accident during a scuffle with his kidnappers, when he had been strangled with the "metal band" he wore around his neck. Curiously he did not refer to a chain as did the autopsy reports, but to a metal band. These comments went almost unnoticed.

At any rate, the communiqué signed by the Dieppe Royal 22nd Cell did not refer to any accident, but to an "execution". And all the physicians who saw Laporte's body agreed unanimously that he had been the victim of a premeditated murder.

Why did the authorities try to give credence to the "accident" theory so long after the crisis, and just as serious doubts were being raised in the press? (When Allmand spoke in the Commons, newspapers were disclosing the Operation Vegas reports linking Laporte with organized crime and the *Toronto Star* was launching its own investigation into the events of 1970.)

Did Ottawa want to rehabilitate some "separatists"? That would have been rather surprising.

Was the cabinet laying the groundwork for a possible alibi for the armed forces and the police? More particularly, an alibi that might explain away the strange circumstances surrounding the discovery of Laporte's body at the St. Hubert base and the unlikely delays that day? An alibi that might also explain why the Rose group never claimed responsibility for the minister's "execution"? That is more likely.

During his first appearance in court, Paul Rose told the prosecutor to ask Robert Bourassa the question: who killed Laporte?

If, as many people believe, the armed forces and the police were in some way involved in the "final act of the Laporte tragedy," could their behaviour on October 17, 1970, be explained by the difficulty of timing their actions to coincide exactly with those that were blamed on the FLQ?

Until the October crisis, the law enforcement agencies were scarcely in the habit of being so nonchalant when it came to unmasking an "FLQ plot". Apparently a "federal crisis" required more planning and care.

It was the "unsatisfactory nature" of the work done by the FBI and CIA that led the U.S. House of Representatives to decide on September 17, 1976, to re-open the official investigations into the assassinations of John F. Kennedy and Martin Luther King.* How can one describe the work of the armed forces and the police in the Laporte case?

What was the real purpose of the order to military bases to watch all cars travelling near the base limits and to record the licence numbers systematically? And this, starting on October 6, 1970.†

* Dispatch from the Washington bureau of Reuters news agency, September 16, 1976.
† CBC, *Background to Military Role*, pp. 11-13.

Certain residents of the South Shore community of Boucherville have said that security around the St. Hubert base was particularly heavy on October 17. *Around 6:00 p.m.,* as they were driving home, to the east of the base, they were stopped *twice* by troops manning roadblocks on La Savanne Road. How could Laporte's kidnappers have driven through these roadblocks in their "hot" car without being spotted by the hundreds of troops who were guarding the St. Hubert base? The official version of this aspect of the Laporte case is simply incredible.

One can imagine the questions that must have occurred to Dr. Prévost and the serviceman who had received the anonymous call at noon, when they learned that a cell named Dieppe Royal 22nd had "executed" Laporte.

Many people immediately made a connection between "Royal 22nd" and the Royal 22nd Regiment, even though that famous unit did not take part in the Dieppe raid of 1942, as *Le Devoir* pointed out on October 19. In the same article, *Le Devoir* reported for the first time that death had been caused by strangulation through the "use of a thin wire." The paper added that the minister had been strangled after being mutilated extensively. It reported that the police did not blame the slaying on Laporte's kidnappers, but on another "cell" that was "in charge of executions."

Still, the authorities lost no time in imposing their version: that the Rose group had kidnapped, sequestered and murdered Laporte without any outside help or support. The media soon forgot the references to the sinister cell "in charge of executions" and the Royal 22nd Regiment.

However, certain policemen (who had been taken in like everyone else since the beginning of the crisis) "tapped" a startling conversation on October 18, 1970, between a highly influential Quebec Liberal and one of his close friends. The Liberal party official confided to his friend that Laporte had not been killed by the individuals everybody had in mind, but by the "authorities".

The minister's associates came to the same conclusion after being excluded from all information and decisions relating to his fate after his abduction on October 10. They became convinced that the authorities had stage-managed the crisis, even at the risk that it would end in tragedy. If this was the case, they felt, "our governments" rather than the FLQ could have made the key decisions.

In a letter to *Le Devoir,* published on October 30, 1970, they wrote: "We who spent entire nights trying to foresee the repercussions of various ambiguous statements, could not believe the frightful destiny that was being built up day by day, hour by hour. . . . Some of us identified the body of Pierre Laporte at the morgue in the early hours of October 18. We would have every reason to be vengeful. But if we were, there would be plenty of time for that . . . . We are all too close to the events to define the judgments about our governments that we want to go down in history."

Since that time, "our governments" have often been urged to set up a public inquiry into the events of 1970. Each time, they have refused, claiming that "the courts have decided," that the case is closed and that everything has been made public.

The Autopsy Reports

How can this case be closed when we now know that on October 17 Paul Rose had been at the Queen Mary apartment for four days and that Bernard Lortie had moved in with friends in Montreal on October 16. Also, according to Richard Therrien's testimony at the coroner's inquest, Jacques Rose and Francis Simard had just been in prison. In fact, Therrien stated *three times* that Jacques

Rose and Simard said on October 17 that they had just come out of prison after being held for two days.

When Therrien overheard this surprising remark, the Rose brothers and Simard were in his apartment on Queen Mary Road in Montreal. They did not appear nervous at all, he testified. Jacques Rose borrowed a new pair of trousers because "he planned to go out with my sister that night." If any of them had murdered Laporte that day, or even if they had witnessed his "accidental" death, wouldn't they have behaved differently? Besides, it was only the next day that they decided to build a hiding place in a closet, after police issued Paul Rose's picture to television stations and newspapers.

Therrien's testimony on November 23, 1970 went largely unnoticed at the time, but it provided significant and intriguing details. Here are some excerpts from the official transcript of the questions by a special Crown attorney and the answers by Therrien:

A. I know that when Francis Simard arrived [on October 17], he joined us in the living room and said he had been inside for two days, along with Jacques Rose.
Q. Inside? Inside what?
A. In prison.
Q. In prison. What did he say then, that they had escaped or had been released?
A. No. That they had been released.
Q. Did they say this seriously or were they joking?
A. No, it was not a joke, it was serious. . . . *
Q. What were they saying at that time? [On or about October 20, 1970.]
A. I know that . . . I remember asking Jacques Rose what

* Transcript of coroner's inquest, p. 472.

connection he had with that [Laporte's death] and he said he had
had nothing to do with that. He said that he had been arrested and
that Francis [Simard] had been arrested, too . . . *
Q. Sir, someone [Jacques Rose] comes to your apartment on the
17th, he asks you to lend him a pair of trousers, and you did not
ask, "What's wrong with your pants? Are they torn? Do you
want to have them cleaned, ironed or what?"
A. I did not ask any questions . . . He said [on October 17] that
he had been inside for two days.**

Therrien also testified that on another occasion, after October
17, Jacques Rose told the occupants of the Queen Mary Road
apartment: "Please stop asking yourself questions. We didn't do
it."† Jacques Rose said the same thing later to Michel Viger,
who hid the Rose brothers and Simard in his farmhouse at St.
Luc.

At a later point in his testimony,†† Therrien said he had never
feared that he would be charged with complicity in the kidnapping or murder because "the War Measures controlled everything."

If Jacques Rose and Simard were in custody on October 17,
why were they released? Had they been interned in the massive
police sweep in the first hours after the War Measures proclamation? Were they holding Laporte at that time and, if so, where?
Just who was left with Laporte on October 17, the day he died?
By that time, if one accepts the statements of the four members of
the Chénier Cell, Paul Rose had been staying in Montreal for
several days, Lortie was with friends, and Jacques Rose and
Francis Simard were in custody.

Despite Therrien's testimony, Judge Trahan did not seek the

* *Ibid.*, p. 499.
** *Ibid.*, p. 510.
† *Ibid.*, p. 517.
†† *Ibid.*, p. 536.

answers to the questions that arose. Jacques Rose and Simard never had an opportunity to testify about their reported arrests and the circumstances surrounding them.

On top of these unanswered questions and all the others mentioned earlier, we find that the autopsy on Laporte's body led to three separate reports. The least that can be said about these reports — dated October 19, October 21 and November 6, 1970 — is that they lend weight to the belief that a total or partial "cover up" prevailed in the Laporte case.

The three reports were signed by two pathologists, Dr. Jean-Paul Valcourt and Dr. Jean Hould. Dr. Jean-Marie Roussel, who was then director of the Quebec Medical-Legal Institute, refused to counter-sign these reports, even though he, too, had examined the body on October 18.

Many people, most of them police officers, were present during the autopsy, which was conducted between 3:00 a.m. and 7:00 a.m., October 18, at the Medical-Legal Institute at the Quebec Police headquarters, 1701 Parthenais Street, in Montreal.

The final autopsy report, dated November 6 — that is 20 days after Laporte died — referred to the presence of the following persons: Corporal René Marchand, Captain Raymond Bellemare and Constables Jean-Claude Boislard and Léopold Bougie of the Quebec Police; Bernard Péclet, Jacques Dansereau and Pierre Boulanger of the medical institute; René Larichelière, an autopsy technician; Dr. Valcourt and Dr. Hould.

High-ranking officers of the Quebec Police and armed forces representatives also attended the autopsy, but they were not named in any of the reports. The Medical-Legal Institute is a branch of the Quebec Justice Department. The department banned the publication of the pathologists' "preliminary" findings until October 21, 1970. No convincing reason for this decision was ever given by Jérôme Choquette.

The most striking thing about the three autopsy reports is that they were drafted in an irregular, not to say illegal, manner. According to a Quebec Justice Department spokesman and several pathologists interviewed by *Le Jour* in 1975, the first or preliminary report must be dictated *during* the autopsy itself. The pathologists dictate their observations and conclusions throughout the autopsy with the help of tape recording equipment. Afterwards, these observations are transcribed fully and they serve as the basis for the preliminary conclusions.*

In the Laporte case, there is no trace of any tapes or transcriptions that would have been recorded during the autopsy, during the early hours of October 18, to prepare the preliminary report that Dr. Roussel did not sign, even though he examined the body.†

What happened to these tapes and transcriptions of the pathologists' findings? Were they destroyed? Are they still stored in the Justice Department's vaults? What were their contents? Did these contents contradict the autopsy report? Why did Dr. Roussel refuse to endorse the preliminary report?

Why did Dr. Valcourt and Dr. Hould wait until the next day to draft their preliminary report? Did they draft it from memory? Why did it take them *twenty days* to write their final report? Could it be because the coroner's inquest was to open the day after the appointment of Judge Trahan and the arrest of Bernard Lortie?

A final question arises: were the pathologists left entirely free to report all their findings?

The three reports relating to the autopsy state that Laporte died of strangulation and that he was strangled with his own neck chain. The wounds observed on the left wrist, the base of the right thumb and the chest are described as "rather superficial and

---

* See the series in *Le Jour*, November 1975.
† *Ibid*.

incapable of causing death.'' (In autopsy pictures introduced at the inquest, however, these wounds look far from superficial.) The final report, dated November 6, stated that these three wounds ''certainly were inflicted before death, at least two hours before.'' This conclusion was drawn from microscopic examination of tissue from a single wound (the one in the chest). There is no reference to similar examinations for the other wounds. In separate interviews, Dr. Jean-Marie Roussel and Dr. Yvon Prévost said that the injuries to the left wrist and right hand were healing at the time of death, which indicates that they were sustained before October 17.

Judging from the November 6 report, the strangulation theory seems plausible at first glance, even though there is no record of an examination of the heart (the weight of the heart is given). At the FLQ trials, however, defence counsel Robert Lemieux described the conclusions about a strangling death as ''a completely false theory'', arguing that the chain the minister wore was too flimsy to withstand the pressure necessary to cause death.

The pathologists set the weight of the body at 178 pounds, while at the time of his kidnapping Laporte weighed 180 pounds, according to a description issued by Quebec Police on October 10. This contradicts the theory that the minister had practically nothing to eat during his captivity and that, as some people claim, he soon lapsed into depression. (The impassive James Cross lost twenty-two pounds during his ordeal.)

The most surprising difference between the autopsy reports deals with the time of death on October 17. The reports dated October 19 and 21 placed this time ''approximately'' *between noon and 11:00 p.m.,* while the final report placed it *between 3:00 p.m. and 9:00 p.m.*

How can such long time spans be explained? Why was the

eleven-hour time span recorded the day after the autopsy reduced to six hours twenty days later?

According to the pathologists interviewed by *Le Jour* in 1975, the time of death can be determined *within one hour* of the actual time, when the autopsy is performed in a twenty-four hour period after death. Even if the earliest estimate of the time of Laporte's death is taken, the autopsy was performed within twenty-four hours of his death.

For the past ten years, all pathologists have been familiar with a remarkably accurate technique to determine the time of death. By taking a specimen of intra-retinal fluid from the body with a hypodermic needle, before transporting the body to the morgue, a doctor can determine the time of death with only a slight margin of error. What happened to the results of this test in Laporte's case? Wasn't it part of the ''special duty'' assigned to Dr. Yvon Prévost by the armed forces? Were the technical data from this test destroyed or concealed along with those from the autopsy?

The pathologists to whom we showed the three autopsy reports agreed unanimously that in Laporte's case, the time of death could have been pinpointed within a few minutes, or within sixty minutes at the most. The approximate nature of these reports reduces considerably their scientific value and raises doubts about their findings.

Disturbing Coincidences

Another puzzle is the number of disturbing coincidences between certain facts related earlier and the various estimates of the time of Laporte's death.

For example, the estimate given in the October 19 report, between noon and 11:00 p.m., corresponds to the time elapsed between the anonymous call received at the Mobile Command communications centre and the arrival of men from the Quebec

Police at the location where the body was found.

The estimate given in the November 6 report, between 3:00 p.m. and 9:00 p.m., corresponds to the time elapsed from the first call received by Mrs. Sasseville at CKAC to the arrival of Dr. Yvon Prévost at St. Hubert.

On top of these coincidences, we have already noted that the final autopsy report was filed on November 6, twenty days after Laporte died and the same day when the justice department named Judge Jacques Trahan as acting coroner in the Laporte case, when police arrested Bernard Lortie, and when Commissioner Higgitt of the RCMP and Solicitor-General McIlraith proclaimed in Ottawa that the FLQ was about to collapse like "a house of cards."

It is very difficult to understand why the pathologists needed twenty days to complete an autopsy report whose main conclusions were already set down in the October 19 document. It is equally hard to understand why Justice Minister Choquette waited three weeks before appointing a coroner. And why police announced the collapse of the FLQ at the same time, one month after the Cross kidnapping, when the FLQ members had been kept under surveillance for at least two years.

It is difficult to believe that all these events were coincidences.

A Perfunctory Inquest

As soon as he was appointed coroner, two hours *before* Lortie's arrest, Judge Trahan told reporters that "justice must be swift" in the Laporte case. And justice was swift. Why was it so important to rush proceedings? To limit the scope of the inquest to the police "disclosures"?

It is a fact that the coroner accepted without question the version provided in the final autopsy report, drafted by Dr. Valcourt and Dr. Hould the day before they testified. Perhaps he had no choice. He accepted in the same way the statement by Lortie, who described it later as false, and, at a later stage, the "complete confession" attributed to Francis Simard by the police, which was unsigned and involuntary and as such would not have been admissible as evidence at a proper trial. Exactly three months after the James Cross kidnapping, Judge Trahan found the Rose brothers, Simard and Lortie "criminally responsible" for Laporte's death on the basis of this evidence. At the same time, the armed forces returned to their bases. Trudeau's functionalism had never proved so spectacularly effective. The *indépendantistes* could not help but get "the message."

Laporte's friends, some of whom had identified his body on October 18, were the first to dismiss the inquest as "a complete farce."* Their reaction was attributed to emotion and spite.

Of course, "very serious doubts" were expressed when Judge Trahan accepted the unsigned statement that police attributed to Simard without first hearing testimony about the manner in which the statement was obtained.† But such criticism made absolutely no impact at the time. Public opinion had already been shaped firmly by the authorities. The "confessions" confirmed what they had stated about the circumstances of Laporte's death. And in time of war, the authorities never lie, as we all know.

The "big tragic show," as Jacques Ferron called it, was stage-managed from high places, in such a way that the scapegoats had few chances to escape conviction.

Escape Attempt, Scuffle, Accident

According to the "police confessions," Laporte was left alone for a moment by his kidnappers and he attempted to escape by

---

* Letter to the editor of *Le Devoir*, October 30, 1970, from a group of Laporte's friends. Full text appears in Trait, *op. cit.*, pp. 186-7.

† For details on this subject see Haggart and Golden, *op. cit.*, chapter 11.

leaping through a window. Instead of jumping through the lower frame and a screen, he aimed at the upper frame and the broken glass caused the cuts mentioned by the pathologists.

Alerted by the noise, the kidnappers supposedly grabbed him from behind, tied him up and bandaged him to stop the bleeding. A few hours later or the next day (the "official" versions clash on this point) they are alleged to have strangled him with his neck chain. They were presumed to have committed this crime in cold blood, for political motives.

All this was said to have taken place at 5630 Armstrong Street in St. Hubert, although police did not find any convincing evidence that Laporte had been held there. In the pictures taken by police photographers after the raid on October 19, the only broken window that can be seen is a front window that had been smashed by the police explosives.

Later — at first unofficially and then officially in the Commons — we were told that Laporte died accidentally during a "scuffle" with his kidnappers. This theory, put forward by Warren Allmand in 1973, was mentioned for the first time in Dublin on December 4, 1970, by Noel Dagg, a brother-in-law of James Cross. Dagg told reporters that he had received this information from "confidential sources." His remarks were reported in many newspapers on December 5.

If this story of a scuffle was well-founded in December 1970, why was it not mentioned in the "confessions" that were later attributed to Simard and Paul Rose? If there really was a fight between Laporte and his kidnappers, were these the same men who were charged with the kidnapping?

In any event, the fact remains that it is extremely difficult for an untrained person to strangle someone who tries to evade or resist his assailants. Dr. Jean-Marie Roussel, former director of the Medical-Legal Institute, said in an interview with *Le Jour* that he believed Laporte's murder was premeditated. He said the murderer must have held the minister face down with his full weight and strangled him from behind while compressing his lungs and thorax.*

In a case of strangulation, death occurs after an interval ranging from four to eight minutes, but asphyxiation occurs within a few seconds.

According to Robert Bourassa, however, Laporte agonized for twenty minutes.† If this is true, what was the real cause of his death?

Some people still claim that he was finished off with a bullet after being tortured. These reports that the minister was mutilated and then shot at close range come from his former associates, and professionals who were consulted after the slaying. Other sources believe that Laporte was garroted with a thin wire of the kind used as a combat weapon in various theatres of war. Questioned about these conflicting theories in 1975, Dr. Roussel replied that in his view the Laporte autopsy reports had the same credibility as "the official ballistics tests made after the assassination of President Kennedy." He declined to elaborate.

During an open line program on radio station CKVL in November 1975, the foreman of one of the juries that acquitted Jacques Rose on charges of murder, kidnapping and sequestration, said that until the trial he attended, the resistance of Laporte's famous neck chain had never been tested scientifically. (Tests conducted at the University of Montreal showed that it took only fourteen pounds of pressure to break the chain, but the prosecution and defence drew conflicting conclusions from these findings.) The jury foreman added that Jacques Rose was acquitted because there was no evidence that Laporte had

* See the series in *Le Jour,* November 1975
† Transcript of Jacques Guay's recorded interview with Robert Bourassa, March 1971.

been confined and murdered in the house on Armstrong Street.*
Other jurors have corroborated these statements. (The jury foreman, who is known to the author, asked that his name be
withheld because he has received threats. The trial in question
was in 1972.)

It should also be noted that the members of the Chénier and
Liberation cells were never wanted for murder. A list of wanted
men published by the RCMP on November 11, 1970, stated that
Paul Rose and Marc Carbonneau were being sought on kidnapping charges, while Jacques Rose, Francis Simard and Jacques
Lanctôt were sought for "conspiring to kidnap." (Bernard Lortie had been arrested five days earlier.)

By coincidence, the day the justice department decided to
publish "preliminary" findings from the autopsy, a
communiqué attributed to the FLQ and dated October 21 stated
that Laporte had injured himself while trying to escape at 10:00
a.m. on October 17. By another coincidence, the autopsy report
made public on October 21 stated that the injuries found on the
body had been caused "at least two hours before death," which
was set approximately between 12:00 noon and 11:00 p.m.

On the other hand, the "confessions" of the alleged assassins
later declared that the minister attempted to escape on Friday,
October 16, without giving the exact time. These "confessions"
do not give the time of death, either. It is as if the people involved
had forgotten. But when someone decides freely to "tell all", he
does not leave out such facts, generally speaking.

In short, the "confessions" seem to have been drafted in such
a way that they would not contradict the autopsy reports.

Until now, the exact causes and circumstances of Laporte's
death have remained official secrets. And many key witnesses

---

*Open line program with host Mathias Rioux, who along with the author
interviewed the juror privately.

have been sworn to secrecy so that they would not threaten "national security".

For instance, there is a man we contacted in 1975 while doing research for a series in *Le Jour* on this subject. We learned from unimpeachable sources that he had been an eyewitness to certain events relating to Laporte's death. What follows is the transcript of the conversation with him, which was typical of several conversations we had then with other witnesses who were afraid to talk:

Le Jour: Mr. X, we know for a fact that you were among those who saw Pierre Laporte's body in October 1970. We would like to meet you to discuss this.

Witness: Sir, this is impossible. *I was sworn to secrecy.*

Le Jour: You were sworn to secrecy by whom?

Witness: I have nothing to tell you. I was sworn to secrecy. If I said two words to you, I know very well that *newspapers in the whole world would report the news.*

Le Jour: Why were you sworn to secrecy?

Witness: If I talked, where would the blows come from? From the government or elsewhere . . .

Le Jour: What do you mean by "elsewhere"?

Witness: I told you I was sworn to secrecy . . . Apart from that, if you understand me . . . I was sworn to secrecy . . . You have the coroner, ask him . . . Don't insist.

More than six years after the October crisis, many witnesses like this man remain terrified. At the same time, a gag rule has been imposed on all policemen and servicemen about "everything that relates to the Laporte case." The research staff of the television documentary *The October Crisis* discovered this in 1975.* Despite their efforts, they were unable to bring about the

* Unpublished research materials for the 1975 CBC documentary *The October Crisis*.

reversal of this rule, which violates the public's right to know. Once more, national security comes ahead of every other consideration.

If Laporte's death had been the work of the FLQ alone, would national security have been invoked to conceal its circumstances and the true causes of the events of October 1970?

An Odd Manhunt

The fact that the October crisis was fabricated offers an explanation of why law enforcement agencies conducted such a strange manhunt in 1970, even though they had never before been so massively mobilized nor so well equipped.

As we have seen, it was decided at a high level, while Laporte was being held hostage, not to pick up Paul Rose. His name was not mentioned publicly until after the minister died. At the same time, the police issued the name and picture of Marc Carbonneau of the Liberation Cell, but not those of Jacques Lanctôt, even though newspapers had immediately linked him with the Cross kidnapping on October 5.

On October 19, police "discovered" the house on Armstrong Street that they had known about for months. On November 6, police raided the apartment on Queen Mary Road (where Lortie was arrested), although the address of that apartment had been found as a result of the raid on Armstrong Street three weeks earlier.

Police did not arrest the Rose brothers and Francis Simard until the night of December 27, even though they had known for at least one month that the trio was hiding in a farmhouse at St. Luc, rented by Michel Viger.

Viger's house had been raided for the first time on October 23, after police had found a panel truck stolen in St. Hubert parked nearby. After this truck was found, Alain Dufresne, a former

Mountie who was police chief for the Town of St. Luc, was instructed by the RCMP and the Quebec Police to watch Viger's house closely.*

When Dr. Jacques Ferron was called on the night of December 27-28 to serve as a mediator at St. Luc, he realized that he was being associated with a "show" in which all the parts had been scripted in advance and allocated without any consultation with the unwitting actors.†

As for cars, only the Chevrolet bearing license plate number 9J-2420 figured in the Laporte case, according to the official version. Still, on the night of October 10, police were looking for two other cars, including a dark green Chevelle with license number IM-1136, in which a Laurentian Autoroute patrolman thought he had seen Laporte and three other men. This car was heading north at high speed. The other car being sought by the police was a Chevrolet that Laporte's neighbors had noticed in their neighborhood on several days before the abduction. The *Montreal Star,* which reported these facts on October 12, stated that police were looking for all three cars, since it seemed clear that the kidnappers had switched cars quickly to evade the roadblocks.

Curiously, it was the "hottest" of these vehicles, the 1968 Chevrolet with license number 9J-2420, that was eventually found at the St. Hubert airport.

The preceding facts certainly do not prove that the members of the Chénier Cell did not play *any* role in the Laporte case. But if they did play a role, we do not know exactly what it was. It is not inconceivable that such a role may have been of secondary importance, compared with that of the powers that be.

The participation of the Chénier Cell members in the kidnapping, sequestration and "execution" of Laporte therefore re-

* *Ibid.*
† *Le Canada Français,* October 10, 1972.

mains to be proven. Contrary to what the authorities have always claimed, the courts have not really settled the issue and have never been given the means to do so.

To win a conviction against Paul Rose, for instance, special prosecutor Jacques Ducros had to resort on March 12, 1971, to this novel argument — that the accused had not "supplied any evidence to back up his denial" that he murdered Laporte! We know today that Paul Rose was not in St. Hubert on October 17, 1970. The same argument was used by the prosecution at the trials of Francis Simard and Bernard Lortie.

In flagrant contradiction of the tenets of Canadian criminal law, it was in that case not up to the prosecution to prove beyond a reasonable doubt that the accused were guilty. Instead, the accused were expected to prove their innocence . . . without counsel and, in Paul Rose's case, *in absentia!*

When Jacques Rose stood trial, much later than the other three and in less perfunctory proceedings, he was acquitted three times by a jury and the prosecution did not appeal. He was finally sentenced to eight years in prison after being convicted of simply helping his brother to escape arrest.

After the Rose brothers and Simard were arrested, Robert Bourassa made some comments that were almost word for word the arguments against separatism formulated in 1964 by Pierre Trudeau: "This is an important victory against individuals who are hostile to our society, against elements that are ready to resort to any form of violence to achieve their ends."

The Authorities Exclude the Laporte Clan

The "important victory" that Premier Bourassa celebrated at the end of 1970 was considered by Laporte's associates to be the triumph of political cynicism.

As soon as her husband's "execution" was announced officially, Mrs. Laporte shunned the condolences of the "existing authorities" and asked them not only to refrain from organizing a state funeral, but to refrain from attending the private funeral she wanted.

Ottawa and Quebec ignored her wishes and turned Laporte's body into "state property" and his funeral into a display of armed propaganda.

Mrs. Laporte learned of her husband's death while watching television. No police officer and no government representative bothered to see her to break the news or even to confirm the television bulletin. She had to call the Quebec Police herself to obtain confirmation.

This gives an indication of the contempt with which Laporte's family and associates were treated in October 1970. This contempt showed through as early as October 10 when the "Laporte clan" was denied access to the positions of power. It was as if the minister's associates in the government and in the Liberal Party were not affected by his kidnapping, and even less by the decisions that had to be made to deal with the situation.

At Bourassa's request, Laporte's family moved into the Queen Elizabeth Hotel. The premier's staff set up shop on the twenty-second floor while the Laporte entourage took rooms on the twentieth floor.

Around lunchtime on October 11, Bourassa spread the word that he was willing to negotiate for Laporte's release. A short time later, Guy Langlois, his executive assistant, went so far as to tell some of the minister's friends: "We are ready to accept all the (FLQ) conditions to save him."* This of course turned out to be completely false.

Bourassa had already advised his closest aides that there would be no negotiations. Antonio Dubé, deputy minister of

---

* Unpublished research materials for the 1975 CBC documentary *The October Crisis*.

justice and a more conciliatory man than his minister, Jérôme Choquette, was immediately cut off from the decision-making process and placed "on the shelf" for the duration of the crisis.

Among those who were tipped off about the government's decision not to negotiate was the future "negotiator", Robert Demers.

On Sunday night, October 11, Bourassa said in a televised address that to govern is to choose. Laporte's friends, as well as Bernard Derome, the CBC French network's top newscaster, interpreted the premier's statement as a refusal to negotiate. They were not mistaken. When Demers was named a short time later as negotiator "for the government side," the Laporte clan was not reassured, since he had been a political opponent of the minister in the bitter Liberal leadership contest earlier that year. The Laporte clan approached former premier Jean Lesage, who came out publicly in favor of negotiations, but his views were not heeded either.

The minister's associates then decided to ask Mrs. Laporte to go on television and radio to appeal to the government. She favoured the idea but felt she should discuss it with the premier first. When she met Bourassa, he assured her that such a step was unnecessary since the release of her husband was "only a matter of hours" away. He told her that police had found the kidnappers' hideout and were merely waiting for an opportunity to rescue Laporte without endangering his life. This was on Wednesday, October 14. It should be noted that Bourassa did not refer to the negotiations then under way, but to police intervention, which the minister feared so much that he wrote in his letter to the premier that it would amount to his "death warrant". Mrs. Laporte took Bourassa's word but her husband's associates and friends remained deeply concerned. Late that night, about thirty of them met in a downtown hotel and drafted a joint statement calling for an acceleration of the negotiations.

After having "reassured" Mrs. Laporte, the premier returned to Quebec, where he announced that "the prior question" of the safe return of the hostages would have to be settled before the FLQ demands could be discussed. This meant in effect that the authorities were again refusing to negotiate. At no time did the premier's office or the Quebec Police inform Laporte's associates about the "progress" of the investigation. The minister's entourage was excluded from all decision making.

On Thursday, October 15, the armed forces were officially called in under the "aid to the civil power" section of the National Defence Act. At 4:00 a.m. on Friday, the War Measures were imposed and the next day, Laporte was slain. Even so, his associates continued to receive promises that he would soon be rescued, right up to the announcement of his death.

After the funeral, which the authorities exploited shamelessly, the Liberal Party offered Mrs. Laporte a Montreal distribution franchise for the Quebec government lottery, so that she could pay off her husband's debts.* After heated discussions, the party withdrew its offer and agreed to reimburse a large portion of his campaign debts in return for the silence of the Laporte clan. Raymond Garneau, then finance minister, later told reporters that the Liberals paid off Laporte debts totalling about $150,000. Jean-Jacques Côté, who had been Laporte's chief fund-raiser in the leadership race, and a few associates obtained a lucrative Loto-Quebec franchise. These backroom dealings were revealed in part at hearings of the Quebec inquiry into organized crime in 1974 and of the Cliche royal commission on the construction industry in 1975, but many aspects of these transactions remain a mystery.

"The heroes of this drama," Laporte's associates wrote in 1970, "may remain split into factions for a long time to come." For the time being, their faction had lost. The Quebec Police

*Ibid.

continued its investigation into the late minister's political organization, in co-operation with the RCMP. The Laporte clan saw this as a politically motivated attempt to blacken the memory of Bourassa's former leadership rival.

Two years after the crisis, police experts on organized crime were still seeking information on the remnants of the Laporte organization. This is confirmed by a Montreal Police confidential document dated July 17, 1972, carrying the file number F-194; it contains the transcript of a lengthy recorded interview between two officers from a criminal intelligence unit and a former Liberal Party official.

Laporte's associates have always felt that he was the victim of a vendetta within the Liberal Party; they do not believe that his "execution" resulted from an FLQ decision. "Being his associates," they wrote in their letters to *Le Devoir,* "we could decipher the phrasing of his letters better than anyone. . . . We could not believe the frightful destiny that was being built up day by day, hour by hour."

When she read the alleged confessions of members of the Chénier Cell in the newspapers, Mrs. Laporte must have wondered about the many unanswered questions. According to an RCMP report, she told friends early in 1971 that she was now convinced that the authorities "had killed her husband."*

From Pierre Laporte to Robert Bourassa

Robert Bourassa's victory at the Quebec Liberal leadership convention in January 1970 left the party deeply divided. The least known of the three candidates, Bourassa won largely on the strength of a concerted drive by the federal Liberals, who were eager to stop both Laporte and Claude Wagner. These two were

---

*RCMP report dated April 22, 1971 and signed by Sergeant G. Houde and Constable J.O.C. Vachon. File number HQ 305-Q-1-097.

in disfavour because they had been members of Jean Lesage's autonomist cabinet and because they refused to knuckle under to the dictates of the Trudeau Liberals.

These divisions persisted after the Liberals' triumph in the April 29 provincial election, despite the fact that Laporte had publicly offered his "good offices" to his young leader. "I hope," he had said, "that he will accept my friendship and see to it that I can serve as his experience." When the cabinet was formed, however, the Quebec Police informed Bourassa, Paul Desrochers and Jérôme Choquette about the "explosive" developments observed by the Operation Vegas unit.

A few weeks later, Roland Laporte, the minister's brother, died in circumstances that have remained mysterious to this day. According to reliable sources, he died in Charles Lemoyne Hospital on the South Shore after suffering a heart attack during a violent quarrel with a powerful member of a rival Liberal Party faction. Shocked by this incident, Pierre Laporte considered severing all his political ties and even discussed his plans with senior officials of his government department. But after some time, he reconsidered and decided to remain in the party and fight. According to some of his former officials, his kidnapping gave his opponents in the Liberal Party an opportunity to "settle scores" with him.

It is in this context that the minister's associates examined the two letters he addressed to Robert Bourassa the day after his kidnapping.* As soon as the first "my dear Robert" letter was made public. Laporte's associates became convinced that his life was in peril and that, in view of Ottawa's intransigent attitude, it was up to Bourassa to "choose between life and death," meaning that he could either act as "Trudeau's valet" or as an independent-minded statesman.

* This aspect of the events of October 1970 was disclosed by the *Toronto Star* in articles published July 28 and 30, 1973.

Laporte's first letter contained several allusions that alerted his friends. He referred clearly to the death of his brother Roland, used the word "health" many times, less than twenty-four hours after being abducted, and warned against "a well-organized escalation" that could provoke a "completely needless panic." These words had an ominous ring to the minister's associates, who knew from personal experience the hard line towards Quebec that had been pursued by the federal Liberals since Trudeau's rise in Ottawa. As they stated later in *Le Devoir,* they read into Bourassa's public statements hints that the authorities would soon resort to a crackdown against the FLQ which would seal Laporte's fate.

By analyzing Laporte's letter in great detail, especially the use of a series of figures, his associates thought they detected a coded reference to the telephone number at Charles Lemoyne Hospital, where his brother had died. They believed that the minister might be held hostage at the hospital (located in his riding and the only one on the South Shore) or in the vicinity.

According to a senior official of Charles Lemoyne Hospital, police searched the building on October 11, claiming that the paper used by Laporte to write to Bourassa came from the hospital. Whatever the purpose of this search, police did not tell the minister's associates anything about it. The latter drove around residential areas near the hospital, looking in vain for possible clues, until October 17. (That day, police raided a medical office building known as *La Clinique de l'est* at 30 St. Joseph Boulevard East in Montreal. An employee had claimed — as she still does — that Laporte was confined somewhere in the clinic.) In view of all the references to health in his letter and the chaotic state of hospitals at the time due to the doctors' strike, suggestions that Laporte was held in a hospital or clinic do not seem far-fetched. (The November 6 autopsy report mentioned that the minister was wearing paper underwear, of the kind used in health institutions.)

"I feel I am writing the most important letter of my whole life," Laporte's first October 11 letter to the premier began. "For the moment, I am in perfect health . . . Ultimately, you have the power to dispose of my life. . . . I cannot see why they should continue to make me die little by little in the place where I am being detained." This is the tone of the entire letter, written only a day after his kidnapping.*

Laporte knew before he was kidnapped that James Cross' life was not at stake. The Quebec authorities had received assurances about this. Despite the diplomat's abduction, Bourassa had gone ahead with his trip to New York. Until October 10, Laporte himself was not too preoccupied over the situation, which he described to reporters as "a wind of madness temporarily blowing across Canada." The strike by the medical specialists occupied much more of his time. He was working with Social Affairs Minister Claude Castonguay on an emergency bill to order the doctors back to work.

What convinced him, less than twenty-four hours after his abduction, that he faced mortal danger and that his fate rested with Bourassa, and not with the federal government even though it had the power to grant or reject the FLQ demands? Why did he use such pathetic language?

"Laporte caught on fast," Jacques Ferron has written. So did his friends. That is why they exerted all their influence within the Liberal Party while the minister was a hostage. On the night of October 14, they appealed publicly to the Quebec cabinet and not to the FLQ. In their open letter on October 30, they warned that history would judge "our governments" and Liberal ministers, without making the slightest references to the FLQ or

---

* For the text of this and a second letter also written on October 11, see Appendix III.

"separatists." Their only direct allusion to the Quebec-Ottawa conflict was to recall that in a 1965 white paper that had been shelved, Laporte had proposed far-reaching changes in Quebec's language and cultural policies. All this indicates that the minister's associates placed his case at a political level far removed from the one suggested by the "confessions" produced by the police.

In his second letter to the premier, written late on the night of October 11, Laporte stated: "I am told that you are already aware" . . . of the possible "arrangements to put the 7 [sic] conditions into force." Was the use of the numeral 7 a signal of some kind? Since the FLQ manifesto had been broadcast, six demands rather than seven remained to be negotiated at that point. Was this a reference to the seven numbered paragraphs in Laporte's first letter? The first letter stressed several times that the police should cease their operations. "This is absolutely essential," it added, since any raid on the hideout would amount to "a death warrant for me." In his first letter, Laporte asked the premier to make sure that police would stop acting "without your knowledge." In his second letter, he wrote: "I am told that you are already aware." Aware of what?

The best way for Bourassa to put a stop to Operation Essay was to accept the paroling of all political prisoners, but this involved exerting pressure on Ottawa and rallying support from all political forces in Quebec. This was not to happen. The triumph of Operation Essay depended on Bourassa's complete submission to federal decisions.

How could Laporte receive assurances from his kidnappers on October 11 that the premier was "already aware"? Who acted as intermediary between the kidnappers and Bourassa at that point? Robert Lemieux was still in custody and Robert Demers was named as the government's "negotiator" only the next day. The premier announced the appointment shortly before midnight on

October 12 and Lemieux was not released from jail until October 13. Demers opened the talks by proposing that two FLQ members give themselves up to act as "volunteer prisoners" until the release of the two hostages.

It seems unlikely that the minister's kidnappers would have shuttled between their hideout and the Queen Elizabeth Hotel on October 11. Other people might have done so, however, while ensuring that Laporte's letters and the Chénier Cell communiqués would be made public by the news media, as in the Cross kidnapping. If this was the case, who were these intermediaries?

And why did Laporte use a literal translation of the English expression "put into force" (the seven conditions) when he knew this phrase (*mise en force*) was incorrect? In English, this expression is often used in connection with the implementation of laws.

It should be noted that after drafting his two letters to the premier on October 11, Laporte was never heard from again publicly. In Quebec, the government kept up the pretense of "negotiations" while preparing the armed forces' intervention. The Bourassa cabinet officially requested this intervention on October 14. From then on, it became virtually impossible for nationalists in the Quebec government to upset the federal plan.

In an interview with political correspondent Jacques Guay in March 1971, Bourassa said that his government had tried to negotiate for Laporte's release "for two or three days." He added that he had personally appointed both negotiators: "I named Robert Lemieux, then for the Liberation Cell I named Robert Demers."* Taken literally, this strange comment suggests that Lemieux was a government appointee in the talks concerning Laporte's fate.

A study of Laporte's letters and the Chénier Cell communiqués — the cell put out *four* statements on October 11

* Jacques Guay interview with Robert Bourassa, March 1971.

and a fifth the next day — indicates that communications of some sort were taking place between the kidnappers and the powers that be over the seven conditions.

A communiqué dated "October 11: midnight" stated: "We reject any negotiations over the substance of the conditions that have not been met." The October 12 communiqué reaffirmed this refusal to negotiate. The Quebec government was being asked point blank to accept or reject the conditions. No ifs, buts or maybes. Did this ultimatum really come from the FLQ? On October 12, the Liberation Cell took a considerably different position. The Cross kidnappers stated in their own message: "The FLQ *reiterates* its two remaining conditions, set out in communiqué number 6 [issued on October 9, the day before Laporte's abduction] — the release of the consenting political prisoners and the termination of searches, raids and arrests."

According to the official version, the Rose brothers and Simard rushed back to Montreal from the U.S., planning a second kidnapping in order to win the release of the political prisoners. We are asked to believe that, once they pulled off the abduction, rather than backing up the Liberation Cell, they turned around and put it in an untenable position by announcing that any compliance with the Cross kidnappers' two remaining conditions would lead to the safe return of the British diplomat but *not* of Laporte. One of the Chénier Cell messages contained this ominous reference to the minister: "The fact that we are committed to return him alive and in good health is already *a very big* concession on our part."

The uncompromising tone of the communiqué signed "Chénier Fund Raising Cell" was reminiscent of the uncompromising attitude of the federal authorities. Ottawa was waiting impatiently for the Quebec cabinet to move in the "right" direction, namely approving the armed forces' intervention and the War Measures Act proclamation. On these issues, Ottawa was in no mood to negotiate.

The question is, who drafted or dictated the Chénier communiqués? Their contents and style provided sharp contrasts with the clear, well-written communiqués from the Liberation Cell. The Chénier messages were full of ambiguities, vague hints and anglicisms — quite different from the October 27 communiqué attributed to Paul Rose (a former teacher), which referred to Dieppe as a murderous trap. In 1970, all the Chénier communiqués were automatically attributed to the FLQ, but was this assumption correct? And then there is the strange name adopted by this cell — "fund raising cell" (*cellule de financement*). Why add this detail? Evidence at the inquest showed that the Rose brothers were so hard pressed for cash in September 1970 that they borrowed $100 from a friend for their trip to the U.S.

In summary, the facts on record fail to prove beyond a reasonable doubt that Laporte was in fact kidnapped, sequestered and murdered by the four men who have been imprisoned in connection with this case, or that they acted alone. The "execution" communiqué signed by the Dieppe Royal 22nd Cell and even those signed by the Chénier Cell are open to serious questions. There is only one aspect of this "crisis" that is perfectly clear — the "implacable logic" of the federal government in pursuing Operation Essay to its conclusion. (In police circles, the case was known as the Cross-Laporte Operation.)

During a press conference he gave on October 15, the day before the War Measures Act was imposed, Robert Lemieux said he had just been informed that police knew where Laporte was being held. Questioned about this a short time later, Robert Demers replied that he could not comment on such matters because they were in the field of police operations. Not a very reassuring answer for the minister's friends.

Members of the Laporte clan have never been impressed by the official version of the events of October 1970. In the light of the facts mentioned here, it is easy to see why they are skeptical.

In the CBC documentary *The October Crisis,* broadcast in October 1975, the host David Halton ended an interview with James Cross with this revealing exchange:

Halton: Who really won in this thing?
Cross: I did. (Pause) Who lost? Pierre Laporte and his family.*

It is a fact that Laporte was the chief victim of Operation Essay. The "well-organized escalation" he mentioned in his first letter to Bourassa was a result of the offensive against Quebec nationalism that Trudeau and his associates launched when they went to Ottawa. Laporte had reason to fear that, after him, "a third [hostage], a fourth or a twentieth" might be sacrificed to national security and the dogma of the indivisibility of Canada. If Bourassa had exerted real pressure on Ottawa to make concessions to save Laporte's life, he would have been branded by the federal authorities as a heretic, a separatist and one of Claude Ryan's sinister plotters. Instead, like the good soldier who aspires to become a colonel, the premier went along with Ottawa and formally requested the proclamation of the War Measures Act. After Laporte died, he cited the slaying to justify the need for military intervention.

It was the events of the October Crisis which destroyed the independence of the Quebec Liberal government of Robert Bourassa. The ensuing years brought a frantic round of massive foreign borrowings and travels in search of foreign investment projects. Quebec became in many respects like the Latin American countries that have been pacified by military régimes in recent years. The Liberals and their friends grew fat during

* Transcript of CBC interview with James Cross, October 1975.

construction of gigantic projects like the James Bay hydro complex and the Olympic Games facilities, but the voters had tired of all the waste and corruption and gave a clear verdict on November 15, 1976. Even the anglophones, long-time supporters of the party, turned against the Liberals.

Pierre Trudeau failed to crush the independence movement in 1970. Now he has lost his ally in Quebec. But he remains determined to thwart Quebec's aspiration by all means, including provocation. Since he believes that the Québécois have no policies, only feelings, he likely will choose again to exploit fear. Will we live through another "completely needless panic," as Laporte put it? It is up to the Québécois to refuse to panic, to remember the events of 1970 and decide that the next time, it won't work.

Organized Crime and Organized Police

Three years after the October "crisis", the Liberal régime in Quebec was rocked by a "second Laporte affair", when newspapers disclosed the links between the Laporte political machine and organized crime figures. Soon afterwards, the *Toronto Star* published a series revealing how resentful and bitter Laporte's old associates remained about Bourassa's hypocrisy and abdication during the turmoil of 1970. Deep divisions reappeared in Liberal ranks, creating a serious threat to Bourassa's leadership.

In September 1973, the premier caught everyone off guard by calling a snap election. He then cooled off the Laporte controversy by asking the Quebec Police Commission to investigate all the allegations as part of its inquiry into organized crime — after the election, of course. On election day, October 29, the Liberals stunned everyone, including themselves, by sweeping 102 of the 110 seats in the Quebec Assembly. The Parti

Québécois won only six seats, but it became the official opposition.

Quebec newspapers began receiving "leaks" that raised doubts about the government's integrity in several sectors. The public hearings on organized crime stimulated heavy publicity concerning the activities of the "Mafia". In the minds of many people, the dividing line between the government and the underworld became blurred. As had happened under certain régimes in the past, the two entities came to be seen as allies. Jérôme Choquette's resignation from the cabinet and the Liberal Party in the fall of 1975 convinced a majority that the government had "many things to hide." Quebec politics took on the look of a grade B western — Bourassa the bad guy chased Sheriff Choquette out of town while the cattle rustlers lurked on the horizon.

In this ambiguous atmosphere, a rumour spread that the two "Laporte affairs" were connected. More specifically, it was said that the labour minister had been the victim of a revenge killing by the underworld, disguised as an FLQ assassination, because he had been passed over for the justice portfolio and had failed to deliver special favours he had promised in return for contributions to his long leadership campaign. A similar rumour had circulated on the South Shore after the assassination.

At the organized crime hearings, certain witnesses implied in late 1973 and the early months of 1974 that the underworld had infiltrated the FLQ in 1970. But they carefully avoided giving any details. Of course, it was general knowledge that Laporte was not exactly a "choir boy". When he was kidnapped, he already had a reputation for "playing rough", as Claude Ryan noted in *Le Devoir* on October 19, 1970.

However, one wonders what organized crime would have gained by ordering his "execution". This would have been the best way of attracting intolerable "heat" from official quarters.

Were the rumours and the "confidential tips" to journalists investigating the Laporte affair diversionary tactics? Were they designed to ensure that "national security" would not be breached at any public inquiry into the assassination?

Certainly, it soon became apparent that the FLQ had not acted alone in the affair, if it had taken the initiative at all. In his October 19 editorial, Ryan observed that the FLQ appeared to enjoy stronger support than "one would have thought." A few weeks later, everyone realized that the 1970 FLQ had been poorly financed and organized. This became particularly clear after the Rose brothers and Simard were arrested in a crude tunnel beneath an isolated farmhouse, armed with a rusty shotgun. Their total lack of resources contrasted sharply with the image of a formidable group with thousands of members and huge stores of dynamite and weapons, which the authorities created at the height of the crisis.

But the atmosphere of censorship and self-censorship fostered by the War Measures Act lingered on after the crisis, discouraging the media from asking too many questions about the roles played by politicians and their forces of law and order. The Québécois, traditionally indifferent to military manoeuvres, did not dwell on the armed forces' activities in 1970.

When the Laporte "scandal" generated headlines in 1973, some observers adopted a new interpretation of the October Crisis that was less damaging for the authorities. They theorized that the underworld had tracked down the Laporte kidnappers' hideout, taken the hostage away and murdered him. They believed that this explained why the body had been abandoned in the trunk of a car (a common occurrence in Montreal's gangland executions); why the Chénier Cell was so interested in fund raising; why many important witnesses were too afraid to talk and why the Bourassa government feared that sensational disclosures might come out at the organized crime hearings.

But the "underworld killing theory" did not explain why the body was found at the St. Hubert air base rather than on some vacant lot. And it did not explain why the politicians in power exploited Laporte's slaying with such cold-blooded cynicism. Besides, this theory assumed that an official cover-up had shielded the underworld and put the blame on the FLQ. If this were true, one would expect the racketeers to have blocked the organized crime inquiry by threatening to expose the facts.

Who but the powers that be could pull off such a brutal show of strength with impunity and minimal risks? Neither the FLQ nor the underworld would have dared to kill in cold blood one of the most important figures in the government of Quebec. Is it not conceivable that the crime was committed by a military or undercover police unit or by an intelligence agency, as has happened abroad? However far-fetched it may seem, the question does arise.

There have been many reports that certain organized crime figures offered to help police locate Laporte and his kidnappers.* This is not surprising since the massive police and military operations had paralyzed underworld activities. It would explain why Frank Dasti promised friends of Laporte on the evening of October 17 that he would help them rescue the minister.**

In the fall of 1970, the racketeers kept under surveillance by the Operation Vegas team did not show any signs of planning to take drastic action against Laporte or any other member of the Bourassa government. On the contrary, they met some of Laporte's aides on September 17 and obtained assurances that they would not have any problems with Jérôme Choquette. Whether these were lies or attempts to buy time does not alter the fact that they obtained assurances.† The circumstances of this

---

* These facts were mentioned in the *Toronto Star, Last Post* and the CBC documentary *The October Crisis*.

** Jean-Pierre Charbonneau, *op. cit.*, p. 492.

† Nick Auf der Maur, *op. cit.*, p. 22.

meeting were described in an RCMP report dated September 17, 1970.

Another RCMP report, dated March 3, 1971, stated that the same racketeers hoped to get the support of Mrs. Laporte because she was convinced that the authorities had killed her husband.* It is difficult to believe that the underworld would have entertained such hopes if it had planned the Laporte killing in an attempt to extract concessions from the government. If such an extreme pressure tactic had failed, what more could the racketeers expect? The 1971 RCMP report indicates that organized crime was then pursuing the same attempts to influence the government that it had before the kidnappings. This would not have been the case if organized crime had infiltrated the FLQ in order to get rid of Laporte, as some people have claimed. In fact, the infiltration had taken place in the Liberal Party. That is why the racketeers reacted angrily to a reference to "the Simard-Cotroni electoral fraud artists" in the FLQ manifesto.†

Claude Ryan, one of the few editorial writers who did not panic in October 1970, wrote that the crisis created an "unprecedented suspense", shrouded in dark secrecy that left many questions unanswered. On October 19, he stated that Laporte's slaying had all the appearances of an assault against the collective existence of the Québécois. He added that, like everyone else, he could not believe that the federal government, to which he gave "a certain benefit of the doubt," was behind this "conspiracy". The day after the imposition of the War Measures Act, Ryan wrote that Pierre Trudeau had appointed himself as the "military protector" of Quebec.

To conceal the real origins and objectives of this "unprecedented suspense", the authorities had much to gain by blaming

* RCMP file number HQ 305-Q-1-097.

† This has been interpreted as a reference to Vic Cotroni, who has been identified as the boss of the Montreal organized crime, and the wealthy Simard family of Sorel that is related to Robert Bourassa by marriage.

the FLQ for everything. Later, they stood to gain again by linking the underworld with the Laporte case, drawing double advantage from the minister's death. In Greece, the Lambrakis assassination was followed by similar propaganda; the slain politician was first linked with "communists", then with "thugs". There, too, the authorities kept switching between the "murder" and "accident" theories to distract attention from their own responsibility in the matter.

* * * * *

In October 1970, Premier Bourassa was in the best position to intervene on behalf of Pierre Laporte and revoke the "death warrant" facing him. But instead of doing this, he converted his cabinet to the Ottawa hard line on October 14 with the help of Justice Minister Choquette and Quebec Police director Maurice St. Pierre. In March 1971, Bourassa said in an interview, "We had to choose between the national interest and the rest . . ."

In October 1975, William Tetley, then a member of the Quebec cabinet, expressed similar views. "After all," he wrote in his weekly newspaper column, "there was only one death. There are no grounds for recriminations."

Sooner or later, the people who governed us in 1970 will have to come clean. They were not elected to fabricate crises designed to consolidate an artificial and precarious "national unity". Unless they are candid, the majority of the voters will become firmly convinced that government is by nature a corrupt and cynical exercise.

The death of political liberty does not flow directly from the corruption of individual politicians. It arises indirectly from the disgust the citizens come to feel for all "grand politics". This high-level politics too often has no objective other than to keep the people in "voluntary servitude", when its purpose should be to subordinate the needs of the state to individual and collective human progress.

4

THE CONSEQUENCES OF OCTOBER 1970

The first political consequence of the federal onslaught of 1970 was to deter the Bourassa government from returning to Daniel Johnson's strategy of asking Ottawa to choose between "equality or independence" for Quebec. For six years, Quebec ceased to have a real government. Federal authorities were able to continue centralizing powers without any significant opposition, transforming Confederation into what looks more and more like a unitary state.

But this triumph of "functionalism", achieved by Trudeau with the help of the armed forces, did not prevent the Parti Québécois from winning the election of November 15, 1976. We can be sure that the new government will never perpetrate a mass shock treatment of the kind we experienced in 1970. Indeed, this government will be the main target if Ottawa unleashes a new aggression in the months or years to come.

Trudeau's dialectical skill at blaming his opponents for his own "dirty tricks" should not be underestimated. The present prime minister of Canada is the most fanatical anti-Quebec politician we have known in our history. Even if he were replaced by Joe Clark in the next federal election, however, this would not prevent the armed forces and the RCMP from exercising their powers of intervention in times of crisis. A report by a study group stated that the federal government should intervene in one way or another, whenever a "real or apprehended" civil emergency appears sufficiently important.

This report, named after General Michael Dare who headed the study group, was tabled in the House of Commons in an edited version on March 12, 1974. The government announced then that it accepted "the main thrusts of the proposals" and that the implementation of specific recommendations was already "well advanced". General Dare, a Montrealer who set Operation Essay in motion in 1970 as vice-chief of the defence staff, was seconded to the Privy Council Office in the spring of 1972 to conduct a study of "crisis management" in the event of civil disorders and natural disasters. The study was authorized by the cabinet on July 22, 1971, but its sweeping terms of reference were not made public until June 20 the following year. General Dare now heads the Security Branch of the RCMP.

Now that the Dare report has become government policy, I doubt whether a new prime minister will adopt a different attitude. Once the government's "French Power" façade has given way to a John Turner or Joe Clark administration, all the James Richardsons in Canada may feel freer to voice their anti-Quebec arrogance. For the time being, however, Trudeau sees himself as "the man of the hour" and in that frame of mind, he thinks he can do anything he pleases, as we saw in 1970.

The View from the Strategic Operations Centre

After the October Crisis, Jim Davey, one of the mandarins in the Strategic Operations Centre, wrote a forty-two page paper entitled "Government and Crisis" in which he advocated permanent "crisis management" machinery. A onetime resident of Westmount and a close friend of Trudeau, he revealed a deep hostility to the Parti Québécois and a fuzzy understanding of Quebec politics in general in this paper. Like Gérard Pelletier in his book, Davey saw a connection between the FLQ and the PQ, even though he conceded that René Lévesque and other PQ officials had consistently denounced the FLQ.

"These distinctions were not clear in the minds of many individuals and the Parti Québécois is by no means a homogeneous group," he wrote. "If it was not infiltrated by the FLQ, it certainly included some people at the time of the October Crisis who were not entirely unsympathetic to its aims. . . . In seeking independence and promoting nationalism, the FLQ shared a common aim with a number of other groups in Quebec such as the Parti Québécois. . . . The acts of the FLQ were the trigger or the catalyst which created an overall situation within which a variety of disparate groups . . . could pursue some common short-term aims."*

Davey concluded that Quebec was "a very fragile society" in 1970 and was "easily capable of being broken." A chain of events was in the making that could have led to confrontations and some incident similar to the Kent State shootings, he argued. "The natural desire is to think that the situation which occurred in Quebec could not possibly happen again and to try and forget it. It is much more realistic to analyze what took place and to see if it is possible to identify the factors that can contribute towards a potential crisis of violence and confrontation in the future."**

Among those factors, he listed the existence of "revolutionary" groups and of other groups who, although they oppose violence, seek change in society and have short-term aims that could be exploited by the violent groups. The inexperience of the Quebec cabinet and the rapid change in Quebec society were other factors in the October Crisis, in Davey's view.† He called

* Jim Davey, "Government and Crisis," paper prepared in 1972 when Davey was an official in the Prime Minister's Office, pp. 30-33.
** *Ibid.*, pp. 36-37.
† *Ibid.*, p. 37.

for more effective police work and deeper examination of potential crises by the federal authorities.*

Davey's justification for the imposition of the War Measures Act boils down to saying that the Quebec government is not like those in the other provinces and that Quebec nationalism prevents the emergence of a consensus in favor of Canadian unity. As Louis Martin put it, the drive toward independence is seen in Ottawa as "a permanent conspiracy against democracy." It would be easy to ridicule the simplistic SOC assessment of Quebec politics, except that it led to military occupation of Quebec in 1970 and could do so again in a future "crisis".

The Dare Report

What is a crisis? When does an apprehended crisis become real?

The Crisis Management Study Group headed by General Dare offered some rather arbitrary and elastic answers to these questions in its report. It defined a crisis as any event or situation which Ottawa regarded as a real or potential emergency, requiring a direct federal response.†

We learned recently, for instance, that the federal government has adopted plans to control air traffic over Quebec from airports in Ontario and the Maritimes in the event of a "crisis"; these plans were disclosed by the Association des Gens de l'Air, which represents Quebec's air traffic controllers. We can be sure that many other secret plans of this kind have been drawn up in Ottawa. By adopting such a loose definition of a crisis, the federal authorities have taken unto themselves unlimited powers of intervention. This should not be forgotten.

Ibid., pp. 40-41.
† Report of the Crisis Management Study Group of the Privy Council Office on strengthening plans for the response of the federal government in natural disasters and other emergencies, foreword.

According to the Dare report, an emergency exists as soon as a "single event" *may* trigger a series of cumulative repercussions.* In such a situation, the federal government must respond quickly. Large-scale planning and strengthened co-ordination between various branches of the government become imperative. This is one reason that Ottawa wants to retain complete jurisdiction over communications, which are regarded as essential in "crisis management", along with data processing systems, operations centres and logistics support.** The report stresses that there are many similarities between wartime and peacetime emergency planning.†

In short, both the National Defence Act and the War Measures Act can be invoked in peacetime to prevent "civil disturbances" and "threats to national unity." The results of Operation Essay helped Ottawa to "improve" its plans for intervention. Many scenarios are possible, but they all have the same aim — preventing a province from weakening national unity.

When the Dare report was made public (in part) the government announced the creation of a National Emergency Planning Establishment (NEPE), supervised by an emergency planning secretariat in the Privy Council Office. NEPE has named an official in each province to maintain liaison with provincial authorities in the planning of "emergency measures". Of course these plans are kept secret.

In the meantime, the armed forces have continued to conduct "civil emergency" exercises in Quebec. In one such exercise, code-named Neat Pitch, sixty-five high-ranking officers, including eight generals, met for two days in a Montreal hotel in April 1972 to draft scenarios for a Mobile Command intervention similar to that of 1970. Speakers included two British Army

Ibid., p. 11-12.
**Ibid.*, p. 13.
†*Ibid.*, p. 16.

officers who gave lectures on military operations in Northern Ireland. After secret documents relating to this exercise were "leaked" to *Le Jour*, Mobile Command headquarters issued copies to reporters at a press conference at the St. Hubert base on April 17, 1974. Military spokesmen dismissed the exercise as "routine", but it came on the eve of the confrontation between the Quebec government and public service and construction unions that led to the jailing of the leaders of the three labour federations.

It remains to be seen, of course, whether the armed forces could rely on full co-operation from the Quebec and Montreal police forces in the event of future confrontations between Ottawa and Quebec. In the 1970 crisis, newspapers reported that some Quebec police officers were considering strike action to protest interference in their work by certain Liberal politicians.*

The Future of Quebec

In recent months, cracks have appeared in the federal government's Quebec foundations. The Bourassa government was soundly defeated and the Trudeau government's popularity has fallen in the polls.† In Montreal, Mayor Jean Drapeau's reign draws to a close. Things have come full circle for the "heroes" of 1970.

But the Parti Québécois' upset victory could result in a strengthening of the anti-Quebec coalition, which is supported by most of the large corporations and the U.S. government. Perhaps the leader of this coalition will change, but this will be a manoeuvre that will not change the basic strategy. We can expect

---

* *La Presse*, November 26, 1970.

† Not to mention the string of cabinet resignations involving Gérard Pelletier, John Turner, Jean Marchand, Bryce Mackasey, Charles Drury and James Richardson and the discontent generated by the "war measures" against inflation.

very tough battles in the campaign for the constitutional referendum promised by the Parti Québécois and in the next Quebec election. The battle could begin sooner with the use of the "destabilization tactics" tested in Chile, even though federal minister André Ouellet piously denied a few days after the November 15 election that this was his government's intention.

It should not be forgotten, either, that the War Measures Act has not been repealed nor even re-examined by the Canadian Parliament since 1970. This statute gives Ottawa unlimited emergency powers whenever the authorities "apprehend" an insurrection or an emergency. The ease with which the federal parties ducked a debate on emergency laws after the October crisis is an indication of their slight regard for the interests of Quebec.

It is impossible to predict Quebec's future with any certainty, even for the short term. The Parti Québécois victory has revived the hopes that the federal government tried to crush forever in 1970, but the upcoming confrontation involves many unknown factors. Certainly, the government and people of Quebec will face a stiff challenge. They will have to unite firmly to fend off the inevitable federal counter-offensive. Will the Québécois give their new government the strong support it will need during the next few years? Or will they succumb to fear and division once more, crippling the most progressive elements in Quebec society and leaving the majority wallowing in confusion?

The deep desire to cast off domination has often triumphed in the history of man, despite the power of the established order. Can this desire triumph at last in Quebec? That is my hope following the historic turning point of November 15, 1976.

CONCLUSION

A Crisis in Three Stages

In conclusion, three main stages can be identified in the 1970 federal aggression against Quebec. They are in summary:

First Stage. On May 7, the Trudeau cabinet decides to establish a secret interdepartmental committee to plan the actions that would be taken "in the event the War Measures Act comes into force by reason of insurrection." Working closely with the armed forces, the RCMP and other branches of goverment, the committee concludes that a political kidnapping, then being planned by the FLQ with the knowledge of the police, would trigger a crisis. The armed forces already have a detailed plan code-named Operation Essay to intervene in Quebec. In September, it becomes clear that the Liberation Cell of the FLQ will soon strike. On September 28, police and military units go on "red alert".

Second Stage. On October 5, British diplomat James Cross is kidnapped. The authorities create a crisis atmosphere in order to justify the invocation of the War Measures Act and the full implementation of Operation Essay. But most members of the Quebec cabinet appear less willing than expected to go along with the federal plan.

171

Third Stage. On October 10, Pierre Laporte is kidnapped. It then becomes easier for Ottawa to get the approval of the Quebec government for military intervention and for the imposition of wartime emergency powers. The Bourassa cabinet endorses these measures on October 14 and the next day, troops move into Montreal. On October 16, the federal cabinet proclaims the War Measures Act. The next day, a mysterious cell named Dieppe (Royal 22nd) announces the "execution" of Pierre Laporte. This raises the question: if the minister had been released, what would he have said about the circumstances in which he was held hostage and about the War Measures Act? Instead, his slaying serves to justify the recourse to this Act and to mass arrests in Quebec, which provoke few protests because of the general state of shock. Operation Essay seems assured of achieving its objectives. The authorities in Ottawa hope that the Quebec independence movement will never recover from the seemingly fatal blow.

With "an implacable logic," as Gérard Pelletier put it, Operation Essay was unleashed with the stated purpose of defending "fundamental rights." From 1969, however, the authorities could have stopped FLQ activities had they really wanted to. They could have dismantled the FLQ's amateurish organization without much trouble. They chose instead to "plant" their agents in its ranks to be in a position to blame certain Québécois for the use of force.

Firmly convinced that Quebec was not entitled to any form of "special status" within Confederation, the federal government "sacrificed" Laporte to achieve its basic ends. These were, in effect, to subject the Quebec government to federal dictates and to eliminate "the separatist threat." Robert Bourassa cooperated without any restrictions in the attainment of the first objective. The Québécois people, wiser than they seem, prevented the attainment of the second.

Six years later, the independence party took over in Quebec in a democratic election that gave it a comfortable parliamentary majority. At first glance, the federal plan designed by Pierre Trudeau appears to have been upset but, little by little, the inevitable confrontation draws nearer. "The crisis is immediate," warned Trudeau barely ten days after the Parti Québécois assumed office.

While in opposition, the Parti Québécois repeatedly called for a public inquiry into the hidden aspects of the October Crisis and the true circumstances surrounding the Laporte assassination. Many facts reported in this book justify such an inquiry.

The repressive nature of the existing political system in Canada constitutes a permanent and serious danger for the Québécois. The October crisis was not an accident of history, but the premeditated execution of a plan whose central purpose was to wreck the hopes of the Québécois for a future as a self-governing people. There is an urgent need to realize this and to act accordingly: first by shedding light on all the events of 1970 through public hearings; second, by avoiding through elementary caution the provocations and traps that the federal government will undoubtedly fabricate in hopes of disrupting the political and social climate in Quebec and subsequently, if possible, attempting to restore the status quo by force.

Readers who have pertinent information or documents relating to the events of 1970 are invited to write to the author, care of James Lorimer and Company, Publishers, 35 Britain Street, Toronto, Ontario.

Appendix I
The May 7 Committee and Its Successors

On December 23, 1971, the Toronto *Globe and Mail* carried a copyright front-page article headlined: "Ottawa Began Look At War Measures Well Before Crisis." On the basis of secret cabinet documents "leaked" to the newspaper's Ottawa bureau, George Bain disclosed the following facts:

On May 7, 1970, the federal cabinet, acting on the recommendation of the cabinet Committee on Priorities and Planning, set up an interdepartmental committee of officials to consider, among other things, "steps to be taken in the event the War Measures Act comes into force by reason of insurrection." This group of officials, which reportedly was headed by cabinet secretary Gordon Robertson, is identified in this book as the May 7 Committee.

Two days before the committee was created, the cabinet Committee on Priorities and Planning had discussed what the Department of Justice called "a preliminary analysis of circumstances in which demands for social change might be accompanied by criminal behaviour, with or without violence." It so happens that at the time, "demands for social change" in Quebec found their principal political expression in the Parti Québécois, which had received nearly a quarter of the popular vote in the provincial election six days earlier, despite scare tactics orchestrated by the Liberal Party. The "criminal behaviour with or without violence" being studied by the cabinet committee was that of the Quebec independence movement, which the Trudeau Liberals from Quebec had sworn to destroy. Trudeau himself had defined this so-called criminal behaviour in the May 1964 issue of *Cité Libre*.

The May 7 Committee met several times during the summer and fall of 1970, according to the cabinet documents quoted by George Bain. However, it did not produce a report for the cabinet Committee on Priorities and Planning until November 20, one month after the War Measures Act was proclaimed and Pierre Laporte died. That day, Trudeau declared for the benefit of anyone who still might not have understood, that his government would not hesitate to pursue a hard line "as long as it takes."

The cabinet studied the report of the May 7 Committee on November 24 and December 1. The second meeting took place on the same day that the House of Commons passed the Public Order Temporary Measures Act (better known as the Turner Bill, after Justice Minister John Turner) by a vote of 174 to 31. On December 10, the cabinet instructed the Justice Department to prepare a "ways-and-means paper on the longer term aspects of law and order," including the development of emergency legislation less drastic in its terms than the War Measures Act. Such legislation was promised in the Commons but it was never introduced.

The May 7 Committee considered not only the imposition of the War Measures Act, but means to strengthen the role of the armed forces and the RCMP in the "maintenance of law and order" and in "assisting" other agencies of government and provincial authorities.

On April 30, 1971, the Turner Bill expired and on the following May 12, the Trudeau government proposed the establishment of a special Parliamentary committee to "examine the kind of legislation required to deal with emergencies that may arise . . . by reason of lawlessness and violence." But the motion died on the order paper after the Opposition introduced an amendment instructing the proposed committee to inquire into "*all* the circumstances anticipatory of and giving rise, or *purported* to have given rise, to the proclamation of the War Measures Act."

Instead of drafting new legislation to replace the War Measures Act, the cabinet Committee on Priorities and Planning decided on November 19, 1971, to instruct the Justice Department to prepare studies on the causes of frustration among individuals and groups that lead to violence; on techniques and structures that provide for non-violent change; on the philosophy and politics of violence (including the New Left and the New Right) and so on. This was followed by the Dare Report on the strengthening of the federal response to emergencies, a response that receives logistical support from the armed forces. And on March 12, 1974, the Prime Minister's Office announced the creation of the National Emergency Planning Establishment without giving details.

In October 1970, the cabinet Committee on Priorities and Planning consisted of the Prime Minister, Justice Minister Turner, External Affairs Minister Mitchell Sharp, Solicitor-General George McIlraith and two other ministers, according to Walter Stewart in *Shrug: Trudeau in Power*. This means that very few elected officials took part in the decision-making process during the crisis.

As for elected officials in Quebec, Premier Robert Bourassa was consulted by the federal cabinet committee on October 6, the day after the kidnapping of James Cross, when it was decided to avoid any real negotiations with the kidnappers while pretending to negotiate, to buy time. According to Stewart's book, Bourassa maintained regular contact with the inner federal cabinet throughout the crisis, thanks to a special "hot line." It appears that at least two other members of the Quebec cabinet were informed of Ottawa's decision to take a hard line — Jérôme

Choquette and Pierre Laporte. This could explain in part the overtones of despair in the latter's letters from captivity.

The May 7 Committee disbanded after submitting its report to the federal cabinet, but its spirit lives on. Exactly six years after the creation of the secret group, the *Toronto Sun* published a confidential memo by General Michael Dare disclosing that federal civil servants suspected of ties with the Parti Québécois had been subjected to security investigations by the RCMP for years.

Robert Samson, a veteran undercover agent with the RCMP Security Branch, was sentenced to seven years in prison in April 1976 after being convicted of planting a bomb at the Montreal home of a supermarket chain executive on July 26, 1974. At his trial, Samson revealed that "anti-terrorist" agents from the RCMP, the Quebec Police and the Montreal police department (about forty in all) took part in a burglary at the office of the *Agence Presse Libre du Québec* on the night of October 7, 1972. In a report he submitted to the RCMP Commissioner after Samson's testimony, Chief Inspector Donald Cobb, head of the force's security operations in Quebec, admitted he had personally taken part in the planning of the unorthodox search. Chief Inspector Cobb, Inspector Jean Coutellier of the Quebec Police and Assistant Chief Inspector Paul Beaudry of the Montreal police received summonses from the Quebec Justice Department shortly before the November 15 provincial election, informing them that Samson's allegation had been referred to the Quebec Provincial Court for a closed judicial hearing to determine whether criminal charges should be filed against them. Judge Roger Vincent presided over this hearing in January 1977 and reserved his decision. (In October 1972, when the *Agence Press Libre du Québec* protested to Justice Minister Choquette that its files and mailing lists had been stolen in a burglary, he gave the pro-independence, pro-labour newspaper public assurances that the RCMP, the Quebec Police and the Montreal police had not been responsible.)

The same Chief Inspector Cobb was co-ordinator of intelligence operations for the 1976 Olympic Games in Montreal. At a press conference on March 23, 1976, he described his task as preventing a recurrence of "the phenomenon known as international terrorism" during the games. He said the phenomenon could take the forms of bombings, kidnappings or political assassinations. Ostensibly to counter this threat, the armed forces mobilized 16,000 men for the Olympics. The commanding officer was General Roland Reid, who co-ordinated Operation Essay in October 1970.

Since the Olympics, the armed forces and the RCMP are better prepared than ever to intervene in Quebec in the event of "criminal behaviour, with or without violence," as the 1970 cabinet documents put it. In this context, Prime Minister Trudeau's comments in a recent television interview about the possibility of violence and even civil war in Canada were not very reassuring. Appearing on the CTV network program W5 on December 26, 1976, he stated: "I would not be the man to lead Canada into a civil war, but I don't say there wouldn't be others who would not want to take up arms, and hence the danger is not one that I am minimizing." Trudeau implied that Canada could slide into the violence of Lebanon, Cyprus, Northern Ireland and Bangladesh. "You start shooting and you don't easily stop," he added ominously.

In the same interview, the prime minister reiterated his determination to preserve a strong central government, meaning that he opposes any meaningful change in the Canadian federal system and favours confrontation with Quebec. He predicted that the Parti Québécois will get "clobbered" in the referendum on Quebec independence, adding that "certain things" can be done in the near future to "make it certain that they will lose it."

Marc Lalonde, leader of the Quebec wing of the federal Liberal Party and the chief federal strategist in October 1970, sounded the same theme in an interview published in *La Presse* on December 24, 1976. He said his party was preparing to launch a formidable counter-offensive in Quebec, in co-operation with other federal parties, the federalist provincial parties and the voters, through "existing organizations or some that remain to be created." He implied that the new government of Quebec will not be allowed to go beyond certain limits and that Quebec is highly vulnerable to unfavourable economic decisions.

The message from Ottawa is quite clear: Quebec has no right to seek independence, nor an economic association with Canada, nor even the least special status in Confederation. Those who disagree want to "destroy" Canada, which is tantamount to "treason."

To what lengths are the federal authorities prepared to go this time around in their struggle with the Quebec independence movement? Do the scenarios now being planned in Ottawa include the extensive use of the armed forces, as was the case in 1970? At present we have no way to answer such questions. Complete secrecy continues to shroud the activities of the May 7 Committee and its successors, the intelligence services in the armed forces, the RCMP and Solicitor-General's department, and all the federal *agents provocateurs* in Quebec.

The time has come to urge the authorities to publish the report of the May 7 Committee submitted on November 20, 1970, so that, in the words of John Turner in the 1970 debate on the War Measures Act, "the full details of the intelligence upon which the government acted can be made public." The public has the right to know why extreme wartime measures were imposed in 1970 and whether similar measures are planned to prevent the people of Quebec from exercising their right of self-determination.

Appendix II
The War Measures Act

The War Measures Act goes far beyond any permanent legislation in the United States, Britain or the other western democracies. To bring the Act into force at any time, all that is required is for the Governor General to sign a one-page document on the advice of the federal cabinet. This proclamation states that "insurrection, real or apprehended, exists and has existed for any period of time therein stated." The proclamation of October 16, 1970 declared that a state of apprehended insurrection had existed in Quebec since the previous day. Under the Act, the issue of such a proclamation is "conclusive evidence" that a real or apprehended insurrection exists. The state of insurrection lasts indefinitely, until a further proclamation brings it to an end.

In short, the Act grants the Canadian government all the powers enjoyed by a military junta, except that in Canada, such coups d'etat are legal. Is there a single democracy elsewhere in the world where an insurrection exists simply because the prime minister says it does? Once the government decides that a state of insurrection exists, the Act empowers it to suspend the Canadian Bill of Rights and to enact any regulations it deems fit to preserve "public order."

This legislative aberration dates back to the outbreak of World War I in 1914. As Ron Haggart and Aubrey E. Golden relate in Chapter 5 of their book *Rumours of War,* federal officials drafted an Act that gave the cabinet "unprecedented powers to run the country as absolute rulers" because Prime Minister Robert Borden could not decide which emergency powers should be incorporated in the bill and which should be left out. The Act therefore gave the cabinet a "blank cheque" to spell out these powers later by executive decree. The debate on the principle of the bill on August 19, 1914, lasted only thirty minutes. Two days later, the bill passed in five minutes. The War Measures Act remained on the books after the war and was proclaimed again at the outbreak of World War II. Nothing of importance in the Act has been changed since, except that a Parliamentary review procedure was added in 1960 by the Diefenbaker government. Under this clause, Parliament debates the merits of a proclamation on the motion of ten members, but this occurs after the fact, and it would take a deep split in government ranks for Parliament to revoke a cabinet proclamation.

It should be noted that the powers conferred automatically on the federal cabinet by the proclamation of the Act prevail over the constitutional prerogatives of the provinces, according to jurisprudence. "The absolute power . . . is general and cuts across all of the basic rights of the provinces," as Haggart and Golden observed.

This means that if Prime Minister Trudeau's recent comments about the possibility of violence are taken seriously, the federal cabinet could decide one day that another apprehended insurrection existed in Quebec. In this event, Ottawa could assume emergency powers in such matters as censorship, arrest, detention, exclusion of foreigners, deportation, ports and territorial waters, trade, transportation, production, confiscation and disposition of property, and so on. Ottawa could also assume powers that are not listed in the Act, under a blanket clause that covers any eventuality.

In other words, the pro-independence government of Quebec

could be placed under a federal trusteeship which would be perfectly legal. In the United States and Europe, such usurpation of power would be unthinkable, but in Canada technically it could be achieved within the constitution.

Why is it that democratic-minded English-speaking Canadians have not mounted any serious challenge against this extreme law that makes a mockery of all our civil liberties? Could it be that they would condone its use against a legitimate, democratic government in Quebec and against the right of the Quebecois people to self-determination? And why hasn't the new government of Quebec called for the repeal of this law so far? The Parti Québecois administration has a responsibility to do so, if only to test Ottawa's reaction.

Appendix III
Pierre Laporte's Letters

On Sunday, October 11, 1970, the day after he was kidnapped, Pierre Laporte wrote two pathetic letters to Premier Robert Bourassa, pleading for concessions to save his life and (according to his political associates) dropping many hints about the kidnappers' hideout. These letters were to be the last from the Quebec minister, whose "execution" was announced on October 17 in a brief handwritten note from a mysterious Dieppe (Royal 22nd) Cell. Translations of these three documents follow:

Sunday, October 11, 3 p.m.
Mr. Robert Bourassa
My dear Robert:

1. I feel I am writing the most important letter of my life.

2. At the moment I am in perfect health. I am well treated, even with courtesy.

3. I insist that police stop all their searches to find me. If they succeeded this would result in a murderous shoot-out from which I shall certainly not come out alive.

4. In other words, you have the power to dispose of my life. If this were the only question and if this sacrifice were to produce good results, one could entertain it, but we are facing a well-organized escalation which will only end with the release of the "political prisoners." After me, there will be a third one, then a fourth, and a twentieth. If all political men are protected, they will strike elsewhere, in other classes of society. One might as

well act now and avoid a bloodbath and an altogether unnecessary panic.

5. You know my own case, which should be borne in mind. I had two brothers. They are dead, both of them. I remain alone as head of a large family which includes my mother, my sister, my own wife, and my children as well as the children of Roland, whose guardian I am. My departure would mean an irreparable loss. For you know the closeness which unites the members of my family. I am no longer the only one whose fate is at stake, but a dozen people are involved — all women and young children. I think that you understand!

6. If the departure of the ''political prisoners'' is organized and carried out satisfactorily, I am certain that my personal security as well as the security of those who would follow will be absolute.

This could be done rapidly, as I cannot see why, in taking more time, they should continue to make me die little by little where I am presently detained. Decided . . . whether I shall live or die. I rely on you and thank you.

Friendly greetings,
Pierre Laporte

P.S. I repeat: have the searches stopped and don't let the police carry them on without your knowledge. The success of such a search would mean a death warrant for me.

Sunday, October 11, midnight

My dear Robert, I've just heard your speech. Thanks, I was expecting as much from you . . . While eating very frugally this evening, I sometimes had the impression of having my last meal.

About the arrangements for the carrying-out of the conditions, they've told me you have already been informed. The ideal would be that the ''political prisoners'' leave as of Monday during the evening or during the night or Tuesday morning.

The remainder should be done at the same time. My friend the

Honourable Jean-Pierre Côté must be told that the situation for the ex-Lapalme employees is primordial. Maybe we could place a certain number of them in CAT or at the minimum wage commission of Montreal or Quebec if they want to.

For the arrangements, discussions, and practical settlement, the people of the FLQ want lawyer Robert Lemieux. They are prepared to give him full authority . . . from his prison if necessary. You may delegate who you want.

Would you be good enough on receiving this letter to telephone Françoise to reassure her and to give her and the children all kinds of good news from me.

You were asking, quite rightly, for guarantees about the freedom of Mr. Cross and myself. You were right. I am ready unconditionally to accept the word of my kidnappers and I ask you to do the same.

Thanks again . . . and thanks to all those who have contributed to this reasonable decision which you announced with strength and dignity.

I hope to be free . . . and at work within twenty-four hours. With friendship, Pierre Laporte.

P.S. You can tell the handwriting specialist that this letter is indeed written by me. P.L.

The following communiqué was found at Place des Arts on the evening of October 17:

Faced with the arrogance of the federal government and its lackey Bourassa, faced with their obvious bad faith, the FLQ has therefore decided to act.

Pierre Laporte, minister of unemployment and assimilation, was executed at 6:18 tonight by the Dieppe (Royal 22nd) cell. You will find the body in the trunk of the green Chevrolet (9J-2420) at the St. Hubert base.

We shall overcome.

FLQ

P.S. The exploiters of the Québécois people had better watch out.

Appendix IV
A Judicial Balance Sheet

The October crisis produced a mass of arrests and legal charges under both the War Measures Act and the Criminal Code.

A total of 497 people were detained under the provisions of the War Measures Act, according to a Parliamentary return by federal Justice Minister John Turner on February 3, 1971. Of these, 435 were later released without charges. The 62 remaining suspects faced a total of 86 charges under the War Measures Act and 19 charges under the Criminal Code. Forty-nine of these persons pleaded not guilty and 13 pleaded guilty.

On July 31, 1971, Quebec Justice Minister Jérôme Choquette issued *nolle prosequi* decrees suspending all outstanding charges against 32 persons.

Sixteen people were eventually sentenced in connection with the Laporte kidnapping and murder. The central figures in these trials were Paul Rose, Jacques Rose, Francis Simard and Bernard Lortie, all of whom were charged with kidnapping and murder.

Paul Rose was convicted of murder on March 13, 1971 and received a mandatory life sentence. He was convicted of kidnapping on November 30, 1971, and received another life sentence.

Rose appealed both convictions. The murder appeal was rejected by the Quebec Appeal Court in a 3-2 decision on February

13, 1973, and Rose refused to appeal to the Supreme Court of Canada for political reasons.

On April 24, 1975 Paul Rose argued his appeal against the kidnapping conviction before the Quebec Appeal Court but withdrew the appeal before the Crown could reply.

Jacques Rose was tried four times. The first kidnapping trial ended with a hung jury on May 13, 1972, with 11 of 12 jurors favouring acquittal. Following a second trial, he was acquitted on the kidnapping charge on December 8, 1972.

His murder trial ended in acquittal on February 22, 1973. He was released on bail to await trial on new charges, including sequestering Pierre Laporte in the Armstrong Street house and being an accessory after the fact in the kidnapping by helping Paul Rose to evade arrest. Jacques Rose was convicted on July 17, 1973, of being an accessory by helping Paul Rose but was acquitted on the other charges.

Sentenced to eight years in prison, he skipped bail in early 1974 while awaiting his appeal, was arrested on June 1 and lost the appeal on June 3, 1974.

Francis Simard was convicted of murder on May 20, 1971, and sentenced to life in prison. He did not stand trial for kidnapping.

Bernard Lortie was convicted of kidnapping on September 22, 1971, and sentenced to 20 years in prison. He did not stand trial for murder.

All four men were found in contempt of court during the various trials and received additional sentences for disrupting proceedings or refusing to testify for the Crown.

Twelve other persons, seven men and five women, received prison sentences for being accessories after the fact or for giving assistance to members of the FLQ (the Rose brothers, Simard and Lortie). The sentences ranged from six months to two years for the 11 who pleaded guilty after plea bargaining. Michel Viger pleaded not guilty, was convicted by a jury and sentenced to eight years in prison.

As for the members of the Liberation cell, who negotiated to surrender James Cross to the authorities in exchange for free passage to Cuba, the federal government has refused to take steps to bring them back to face charges which were laid against them as a result of their involvement in Cross's kidnapping.

Five members of the Liberation cell and two relatives were flown to Havana aboard a Yukon military aircraft. They were Jacques Lanctôt, his wife Suzanne, and their son Boris; Jacques Cossette-Trudel and his wife Louise; Marc Carbonneau and Yves Langlois. After completing their investigation into the Cross kidnapping, Montreal police filed a total of 33 charges against the four men and Mrs. Cossette-Trudel early in 1971. Warrants for their arrest were issued across Canada and through the Interpol network, in case the group left Cuba. In 1974, the Lanctôt couple, Carbonneau and Langlois flew to Paris via Prague and were given thirty-day residence permits, which have been renewed every month since. When this news broke on June 24 during the 1974 election campaign, Justice Minister Otto Lang immediately announced he would seek the extradition of the exiles. He was overruled by Prime Minister Trudeau. The Prime Minister told reporters: "It is not our government's plan to take any action to obtain extradition. I think the attitude of the Canadian people is that we don't want them back." The next day he added that the FLQ members had been promised safe conduct out of the country and that the government did not want "big open trials" about the Cross case.

Both Conservative leader Robert Stanfield and NDP leader David Lewis demanded that the terms of any secret agreement with the exiles be made public, but the Prime Minister insisted that no such agreement existed. Commenting on the question on July 4, 1974 in a campaign speech in St. Jerome, Robert Stanfield said he considered it imperative to shed light on the government's refusal to extradite the Cross kidnappers. "The truth must come out in the open as to the motives which make Mr. Trudeau so evasive on this subject," he said.

The following August 6, the Cossette-Trudel couple arrived in Paris and were given the same status as the other exiles, after promising to refrain from any political activity. Their application for refugee status was rejected by a French administrative court in 1975.

About the Author

Pierre Vallières was born in 1938 in Montreal, the son of a railway mechanic. In the early 1960s, he contributed many articles to *Cité Libre,* the monthly review founded by Pierre Trudeau and Gérard Pelletier. After a brief stint as co-editor, he resigned in 1964 in an editorial board dispute over the issue of Quebec independence. During this period he was a foreign news editor and union officer at *La Presse,* Quebec's largest daily newspaper.

In 1965, Vallières became increasingly active in left-wing groups and then went underground as part of a new wave of the FLQ. Following a series of violent incidents attributed to the FLQ he and Charles Gagnon were arrested in New York in September 1966 while demonstrating in front of the United Nations building. Deported back to Canada, the two men spent more than three years in prison, fighting highly publicized court battles that ended in acquittals or appeal victories on the main charges, although they were convicted of contempt of court.

While in custody Vallières wrote *White Niggers of America* which has since sold more than 100,000 copies in five languages and earned him a reputation as the "theoretician" of the FLQ. The FLQ in fact never had a central leadership or strategy. In one of its judgments, the Quebec Appeal Court indicated that Vallières in effect had been put on trial for his political beliefs.

Released on bail in May 1970, Vallières spent the summer at a friend's cottage recuperating from the effect of his years in holding cells at the Quebec police headquarters. He did not know the members of the 1970 cells of the FLQ that claimed responsibility for the kidnappings of James Cross and Pierre Laporte.

Minutes after the proclamation of the War Measures Act on October 16, 1970, he was interned with about 250 other Quebec political activists. He was later charged with joining in a seditious conspiracy with Charles Gagnon and three other prominent radicals, Robert Lemieux, Michel Chartrand and Jacques Larue-Langlois. In February 1971 a Quebec Superior Court judge quashed these charges on the first day of the trial because they omitted essential particulars and covered a period of three years. The Crown filed slightly different charges of seditious conspiracy, but Gagnon and Larue-Langlois were soon acquitted and Vallières was released on bail in June 1971. One month later all the remaining conspiracy and War Measures Act charges were dropped.

In October, 1972 Vallières received a one-year suspended sentence after pleading guilty to three charges of counselling criminal acts in fiery letters he wrote from his prison cell in 1968. In *L'urgence de choisir (Choose!)*, published in 1972, Pierre Vallières rejected terrorism and endorsed the Parti Québécois as the only generally acceptable political instrument to bring about the independence of Quebec. Since then he has worked as a community organizer in Mont Laurier and as a journalist for *Le Devoir* and *Le Jour*, and is now a part-time lecturer on communications at the University of Sherbrooke.